Andreas Andreadis

The Origins
of the Greek Public Debt

"une lamentable histoire"

Edited by Alberto Palazzi

GogLiB

ISBN: 9788897527084
First English Edition: April 2012
Copyright © GogLiB, 2012, www.goglib.com
Copyright © il glifo, 2012, www.ilglifo.it
National Bibliography Number: urn:nbn:it:ilglifo-9318

Original Title:

ΙΣΤΟΡΙΑ ΤΩΝ ΕΘΝΙΚΩΝ ΔΑΝΕΙΩΝ

ΥΠΟ ΑΝΔΡ. ΜΙΧ. ΑΝΔΡΕΑΔΟΥ

Υφηγητού της Πολιτικής Οικονομίας και Δημοσιολογίας εν τω Εθν. Πανεπιστημίω.

Διδάκτορος του Δικαίου. Διδάκτορος των Πολιτικών και Οικονομικών Επιστημών.

Lauréat της εν Παρισίοις Νομικής Σχολής.

ΕΝ ΑΘΗΝΑΙΣ ΤΥΠΟΓΡΑΦΕΙΟΝ "ΕΣΤΙΑ,,
Κ. ΜΑΪΣΝΕΡ ΚΑΙ Ν. ΚΑΡΓΑΔΟΥΡΗ

1904

English translation by Alberto Palazzi and David Moadel, © 2012

Contents

Editor's Introduction

Yesterday and today

At the end of the winter of 2012, we resurrected a book written in 1904 that tells the story of the Greek debt from its absolute beginning in 1824, translating an essay well-documented and unique, yet forgotten. Andreas Andreadis's book is a unique opportunity: It tells us the story of the development of an unsustainable system of public finance from its cradle. It is a story that we can only read in such detail here, because the many reports and stories of nineteenth-century Greek Independence War that have been written mention the financial aspect of the story only through hints. Thus, given the absence of any archival records, we will see throughout the text the unique sources the author has drawn on to get the details of this story.

In 2012 this book, though more than one hundred years old, is also a modern book in its own way because the situation in which Greece cannot meet its financial commitment has presented itself again. Now we do not know if the new Greek state failure will be addressed in a civil manner by foreigners (those that Andreadis would call the Protecting Powers), or if it will happen more dramatically, in the form of a disordered default. Nor do we know how many years the crisis will drag on yet, nor how and when we will consider it resolved financially, nor what kinds of burdens and mortgages it will leave to the Greek economy. In any case, we can call the outcomes once more "une lamentable histoire," as it was qualified by a French businessman, traveller and philellene, who analyzed with insight and precision the Greek economy back in 1847, and whom we will meet often in this book.

Given the situation today, some — very few — will enrich themselves and many others will lose the game, not so much paying the bill on the enrichment of a few, but due to the impairment of Greek economic development, and due to the eternal depression that follows each stage of the "lamentable histoire." Except this time, the Greek society will take the opportunity to take a step forward in the slow process of liberation from the custom of political patronage and tolerance of tax evasion.

Today as then, the story of Greek public finance has an individual character that distinguishes it, and which makes it a separate chapter: in the nineteenth century as in 2012, when the many bank and state potential insolvencies in the world seem about to be reabsorbed — but not the Greek one.

The financial crises of the first decade of our century have manifold origins: labour low salaries resulting in individuals' propensity to consume on credit; the housing bubble; speculation about complex financial instruments such as derivatives by persons unfit and unable to understand their nature and risks; in some countries, excessive deregulation of banking activities determined by the disregard of the reasons for the existence of complex banking laws developed during the twentieth century; and a strong tendency in public short-sighted and short-term policies, having received consent from public opinion. Faced with this situation in which a context of distinct pressures determined the critical events, the Greek crisis is actually quite straightforward and simple: First, there was a conscious and intentional government deficit policy to stimulate consumption — a policy conceived in such bad faith as to resort to false accounting entries — and there was consensus of society, vitiated by the distribution of income in this model. Then when it came time to repair the situation through net decisions, the social consensus has left the government and moved on to the idea that Greece might have the time and could afford the luxury of unlimited polemics, international and domestic, rather than arrive quickly to drastic choices. This has progressed to the point that in today's newspapers, and perhaps even in the same issue, we can read poll projections that give the 45% of votes to extremist parties willing to abandon the single currency and even the European Union, and polls that say that 75 or 80% of Greek society is well convinced of the need to remedy the situation at all costs, conscious that the abandonment of the European consortium would cost Greece the return to a rudimentary economy. Such answers are not coherent: It is evident that there are now a good number of Greeks who do not know what to think, to the point of giving contradictory answers when questioned on the same day, or more likely who on one hand understand the ruinous implications of the abandonment of Europe, but on the other hand have accumulated so much hatred and contempt against the institutional parties of their country to think now of punishing them by giving the vote to the proponents of the childish and unrealistic denial of the problem.

Today, if things will settle down, it seems that the Greek people will be subject to limitations of sovereignty as they were for the same reason in 1897, when the International Economic Control (Διεθνής Οικονομικός Έλεγχος, ΔΟΕ) was established — an entity that had an office in Athens in which foreign personnel controlled that Greece complied with the conditions necessary to extinguish a bit at the time the loans borrowed by creditor governments, which at that time were England, France, Austria, Germany, Russia and Italy.

It is clear that the solution of the problem, then, was the post-war inflation and the devaluation of all currencies after the world wars. The International Control literally exercised his duties only until the First World War, forcing Greece to accept the imposed conditions, which included the use of certain taxes and public revenue sources to meet its commitments. Between the two wars it had a marginal advisory role, but it also survived the Second World War, and became extinct after the long agony that the timing of international bureaucracy inevitably inflicts to all its institutions: It being at that time totally unnecessary, documents of the British Foreign Office advised the dismantling of the International Control in the early '60s, but the final consensus of all involved parts for its termination came only in 1978.

Our author, Andreadis, in 1904 intended to tell the whole story, including the then highly contemporary institution of International Control, which existed in its eighth year while he was writing, but the first volume of the story translated here is the only one that was written. It tells us the two oldest stories: the one of the *Independence Loans* that the Greek provisional government contracted with the private market in London in 1824 and 1825 — without any interference of European Governments — and the one of the reckless entity loan that the government of the new kingdom of Greece contracted after 1832, thereby remaining indebted to the three protecting powers: England, France and Russia.

For many reasons, not the least because it gives us a vivid perception of the dynamics of internal disintegration in society and politics in Greece that the problem produced, it's worth reading the *lamentable histoire* of this part of the story. Nevertheless, it mainly deserves to be read because it affords us the unique opportunity to understand in detail the structure of a phenomenon of financial catastrophe reduced to its skeleton, almost as if we had made a culture in vitro of its germ.

Technical note to understand the book

With regard to monetary units mentioned in the book, it is necessary to remember that a *Franc* throughout the nineteenth century, and until the First World War, was tantamount to a twenty-fifth of a *Pound*, as established by Napoleon. Under the term *écu*, it was intended a five-Francs unit, and five Francs were equivalent to one U.S. dollar in the decimal system. However, in the text we find the expressions *Taler, Dollar, Spanish Dollar, Spanish Piastre, Florin, Piastre* and *Distele*, which are all synonymous with each other, and which require explanation. In the ancien régime and until the early nineteenth century, the international currency of reference in both Europe and the Ottoman world was the *Spanish Dollar*, or *Piece of eight*, which had many names: in Spain *Peso fuerte, Peso duro* or *Dólar español, Thaler* in German world and in English *Pillar dollar*, meaning "dollar of the Pillars of Hercules," and therefore in Greek *Distele* ("two-columns"). This coin for a long time was tantamount to a fifth of a Pound, so that the Spanish dollar could be considered equivalent to a French écu when we are only interested in orders of magnitude; the ratio cannot be indicated exactly because the title and the weight of metal changed over time as the exchange rate actually practiced by bankers and money changers. This Spanish currency from seventeenth century was taken as a reference base also for the Ottoman Piastre, whose name in Turkish was *Kuruş* and in Greek *Gròsi*, and that was the monetary unit used in the Greek Independence War until the establishment of the national currency at the end of it. However, since the Turkish currency during the first half of the nineteenth century was subjected to a continuous depreciation due to the coining of *Kuruş*'s having title and weight increasingly reduced (until the Sublime Porte did not supply a currency reform in 1844), it is difficult to say exactly how the Gròsi actually circulating in Greece in the 1820s were exchanged, as mentioned in the text. Certainly their value was much less than the value of a écu, and probably it was a sixtieth of a Pound; it was less than one-tenth of the nominal Spanish Dollar — this is deduced from Chapter A.1 of our text, where it is reported that according to a contemporary writer, Thomas Gordon, 5,587,000 Piastres amounted to 93,000 Pounds in 1825[1]. The value of a Piastre estimated in this way gives rise to probable values in the context of the book.

As for the national currency of Greece, between 1828 and 1832 the new state adopted the Phoenix as its currency (φοίνιξ), of unstable value and difficult to accept as payment, but nominally equal to one-sixth of a Spanish Dollar, so it took 1.1168 Phoenices to buy a Franc, and 28.12 for a Pound. From this it seems clear that a Piastre, or Grosi, circulating at the time of Independence should be equivalent

---

[1]Andreadis's quote is accurate and easily verifiable, because Gordon's book is available in PDF through *Google books*.

to 5.37 Francs, but it is not so because the Phoenix was defined on the basis of equivalence with a theoretical Spanish Dollar or Kuruş, not with Turkish Piastres actually circulating at the time, which were worth much less.

The Bavarian monarchy changed its name to Phoenix, calling it Drachma, but did not change its definition based on the nominal Spanish Dollar and on the theoretical value of the Kuruş. In 1868, the New Drachma was introduced, and this was made equal to one Franc (and even to an Italian Lira, which was always defined on the basis of the French Franc).

As for the purchasing power of this money, we know that over the generations it has become increasingly difficult to determine the conversion rate between currencies, as the relationship between the prices of different types of goods and services has changed over time following the structural changes of production techniques. However, to get an idea of the absolute values mentioned in the book, we can remember that with a Franc at the time of Hugo and Balzac one could, in France, eat a small meal, and with 5 or 10 cents one could send a letter, so one Franc might be considered equivalent to ten Euro today, and one Pound equivalent to 250 Euro. This was in France or England; the value of money in Greece was immense: Consider that in chapter B.3.2 of this book an annual pension of twenty Drachmas is discussed, along with another of less than ten, and only the latter is qualified by the author as insignificant.

Andreadis's text

Andreadis's book is written in the artificial and archaic version of modern Greek created in the late eighteenth century, the now-obsolete *katharevousa*. My translation eliminates several verbose phrases that sounded "...to confirm the reader that we do not exaggerate now let us say the most important thing, namely that..." and eliminates other superfluous phrases (as determined by combinations of many redundant synonymous words), yet is faithful to the content. Being archaic and annoying, I deleted the *plurale humilitatis* often (but not always) used by the author, and in the English version I translated his French quotations. The English quotations generally were not translated in the Greek text.

Curiously, in the original text the chapters are skeletal, and the interesting narrative is almost all in the numerous and extensive footnotes. For example, pages 8 and 9 of the original contain just a single line of text, as they are occupied by long and useful notes that explain what was stated on page 7. Maintaining this approach would result in a text uncomfortable to read, and even more so in an e-book. Thus, I integrated the author's notes into the text sequence, leaving in the footnotes only the references identifying the quotations, as well as some of his literary embellishments and certain of its incidental observations really interesting only to those living in Greece in 1904 (being contemporary and countryman). This forced me to put some words here and there to serve as a connection between the notes of the author and his text, without changing the meaning of the whole. I left in the text pages devoted by the author to the description of the sources, since the character of the sources contributes to the contextualization of the same events narrated: The nature of the events, which consist of the failure of rational decision-making processes that were designed, but were prevented from being realized by a Babel of languages and conflicting mentalities, makes the proliferation of contemporary memoirs and polemical writings a part of the events themselves.

Where not indicated otherwise, the footnotes that remain are of the author; these may be ignored by the reader who does not have the intention to continue to delve deeper than that into the matter. Because the notes are intended solely for people who want to pursue the matter, I did not transliterate the Greek author's citations, as the transliteration would be more of a hindrance than a help to anyone who wants to go in search of the Greek works cited. I kept the dates with the dual display according to the Gregorian / Julian Calendar — for example, 2/14 October 1863 — where the author expressed them in this way.

The reason to read Andreadis's book today is to learn in detail the story of the birth of the public debt from tabula rasa of a country that, until a moment before, had no relations with the articulated and developed financial economy of the European world. Therefore, I have considered first and foremost the need to make the story narrated understandable, which I have done *by inserting some lines of text in italics for clarification* so that there will be no need to report them as editor's notes.

History of public debt (1904) – Introduction

"C'est une lamentable histoire que celle de la dette hellénique" — "It is a mournful story, that of Greek debts": With these words, Casimir Leconte began his study of the Greek government debt fifty-seven years ago. This discussion was part of his *Étude Économique de la Grèce*[2] of 1847, and that is the most complete work that has been written so far on the economy of our country, written by a man who had lived in it for two years. Leconte talks mainly about the Sixty Million Loan contracted after the Independence, while loans contracted during the Independence War are just mentioned in hints, because at that time they were neither recognized nor accounted in the budget, as we shall discuss in detail.

After almost six decades, those who undertake to study this subject can only subscribe once again to that expression, which rather could be blamed for excessive moderation. The history of the Greek national debt is the story of a failure, but it is necessary that we write quite frankly the story of the failures of a nation[3] no less than we write of its successes.

Moreover, in our present world where the sovereign debt is one of the most important problems for Governments, a scholar of financial matters certainly cannot neglect that important branch of finance that is the public one[4]. Therefore, after much research done on the topic of the public debt of Greece[5], the idea of this study as a self-sufficient work came into my mind as a result of the tragic events of the summer of 1897. Since then, I have never ceased to gather

---

[2] At pages 174-187.

[3] If it is true that "as a scholar of his own story people are the best judge of present things and of their fate and fortune": aphorism of Guizot that Paparrigopoulos used as the epigraph of his *History of the Greek Nation*.

[4] See my *Introduction to the teaching of Science of Finance*, page 30.

[5] Public debts have been the subject of my classes in the second half of the previous academic year. In the first semester, I dealt with the general theory of debt, while in the year 1902-1903 I studied the general principles of finance, and of government spending and the tax system in force in our country. A small part of these courses is published in French under the title: *L'impôt direct en Grèce et son évolution*.

materials, and thanks to a stay in England, I was able to draw on a wealth of information from a private collection of documents, a unique opportunity to bring order into the great mass of existing data pertaining to Eastern affairs.

The difficulties of the work were evident: more than anything else, the lack of official publications, and previous studies that were minimally detailed and accurate. Yet another source of difficulty was the choice of topics to discuss, because while on one hand it was impossible to exclude completely the historical events that explain the mode of negotiations and the signing and subsequent management of borrowing by the government, on the other hand there was the danger that the history of the Greek debts would turn into a new political history of Greece. Since the beginning, I did not sufficiently take this danger into account, so this study reached such dimensions that subsequently it took six months to reduce it to the appropriate size. Working on it for the entire summer, I restricted the book to the present limitations; then, having arisen the new fear that the work now appears too concise, I have added these few words of introduction by way of apology.

* * *

The history of Greek debt is divided into three periods:

a first period, which extends until the coronation of King George in 1863[6] and that includes the history of the Independence Loans and public debt of the Bavarian dynasty;

a second one, which begins with the dynastic change and ends with the forced reduction of debt in December 1893;

and *a third one*, including negotiations for settlement and the subjugation of Greece to the International Control, and the facts of war in 1897.

The first period is the one this book tells the story about: the unique and somewhat heroic story of borrowing abroad by the government of the Greek Independent state at the dawning era of its existence, and the other, more melancholic and mediocre story of the debts at the time of the regency of the kingdom of Bavaria and Othon I Wittelsbach. Regarding the other two periods, there is a brief summary in the conclusion of the editor.

The second period can be divided into two phases of roughly the

---

[6] Year in which George I of Glücksburg succeeded the deposed Othon I Wittelsbach, the king of the dynasty known as the *Bavarian* in the text (Editor's note).

same length, the first of which knew only internal debts, while the second began when the gates of European stock markets were opened to Greek bonds and allowed the stipulation of many government loans, among which almost all of the important ones were contracted abroad. The study of the third period and of the negotiations for the transaction will require the study of the establishment of the International Control, as well as the comparison of the situation in Greece with that of other states where the economy was recently placed under international protection in a more or less severe way. These three periods correspond to the three parts of this work.

As already indicated in the introduction, there is no trace of the existence of volumes after the first one translated here.

Finally, in fulfilment of a pleasant duty, I express my gratitude to everyone who contributed to this study by providing information and advice, and especially to my two faithful friends, the Parliament librarians Razis and Kalogeropoulos.

Athens, 20 September 1904

A. The Independence Loans (1824-1825)

A. The Independence Loans (1824-1825)

A.0. Sources of research

The text indicates precisely the available known sources. I have used these bibliographic notes by way of introduction, as the character of the sources is in itself information on the issue of Independence Loans.

The Independence Loans are divided into two periods: the one in which they were concluded and used, which lasted three years, and the one of their settlement through transactions with creditors, which extends over many decades. In the study of the first period, we encounter many difficulties. First, there are no specialized treatises of the theme, since the *Memory about Anglo-Hellenic Loans* in thirteen pages of N. Koresios can hardly be considered such, containing the mere reproduction of some articles which appeared in the newspaper *Merimna*. Then there are some official documents published by the Greek government, but of little importance. Since the governments of the Powers never did interfere in Independence Loans, we also lack any official foreign document (English documents would be useful), while the foreign documents are extremely useful for the study of later Greek loans.

Even the general histories offer us little help, because, for reasons discussed below, those who wrote largely about the Independence ignored the economic side of the story. In the literature on the Independence, there are scattered hints by Finlay, Trikoupis, Blaquière, Mendelssohn-Bartholdy and Gervinus, hints that are more numerous in the first of these authors, safer in the last of them. Additionally, some interesting information relating to two loans that were not concluded, one of which had to be granted by the Knights of Rhodes, and the other which was to serve the defence of Missolonghi, can be found in the book of Jourdain (*Mémoires Historiques et Militaires sur les événements de Grèce*) and that of Fabre (*Histoire du Siege de Missolonghi*). Finally, the *Archives of Dionysios Romas*, published by Kampouroglos, contains some disparate information about loans in general and reveals certain details, hitherto unknown, relating to attempts to find credit in Italy.

All of these sources could provide just the material to put together a brochure for no more than a few pages, like the one quoted by Koresios. However, the misuse of the money of Independence Loans caused countless rumours and slanders, and they engendered long judicial trials in Greece and extensive press reports in England. So, thanks to the records of Greek trials and of English press, I managed to get enough light on the subject.

In Greece, the important trials were those in which Louriotis and Orlandos had to defend themselves. These two individuals of dubious ability — but, I think, immaculate honesty — were sent to England in search of loans as representatives of the Provisional Greek Government. The unfortunate use of the second loan attracted the general indignation on them, and at end caused a decision of the Court of Auditors (however, never executed), which declared them jointly liable to the Treasury of the sum of 809,008 Drachmas.

The newly constituted Greek state was endowed with a complex of institutions modelled on contemporary France; these institutions were mostly just embryonic and inefficient, with tiny staffs. However, there was a Court of Auditors (Ελεγκτικόν Συμβούλιον), similar to the French and Piedmonts' Cour des comptes at least for the definition of its Powers.

By appealing against this judgment in 1839-1840, Orlandos and Louriotis published a giant book in two volumes, 529 pages in quarto, entitled *Apology*, and that is simply the collection of all official and unofficial documents that were in the hands of two authors. So, instead of containing actual apology, the work contains all correspondence between the government and its commissioners, largely related to loans, but also on any matters pertaining to the official tasks of the two authors. So, this source is also less useful than expected, as it is missing a method and a rational design. At least I, reading this *Apology* entirely ten times, could not figure out which thread the two authors followed in writing it, why they introduced certain documents, and why they put some others in that position instead of in the one that would seem to anybody the most pertinent.

There is much more method in the memoir which Spaniolakis published in response and controversy against Orlandos and Louriotis (*Observations on the Apology of Orlandos and Louriotis*, 1840), which is much shorter (84 pages), but contains valuable information missing in the *Apology*, especially in the annexes.

And this is all about Greek publications. But the reprehensible squandering of the money of the second loan also gave rise to the indignation of philhellenes in England, who while investigating discovered that their compatriots administering the resources of the loan were primarily responsible for the waste of sacred money. Then the indignation of the public came to a head and provoked the reaction of many British newspapers, especially *The Times*, which led the most detailed investigation uncovering other scandals and bringing to light things that, without that investigation, would be ignored forever. Many of the things written in London were then translated into Greek and entered in the *Apology*. As the time went by, the scandal of 1825 and '26 were forgotten, but there remained in Europe the persuasion of the bad faith of the Greek government, which squandered the first loan and then failed to acknowledge being the debtor of it. Later, to correct the ideas of the British public and Parliament and to help reach a fair agreement, Gennadios collected and published the most important articles published at the time of the loans under the title: *The Greek Loan of 1824 - 1825 - How They Were handled and what the world thought of* (London, 1878). In the following, the reader will find numerous references to this collection of articles.

Finally, it should be noted that most of the second loan money was spent in the construction of warships in the United States. The contract of these ships necessitated Kontostavlos' mission in America, followed by legal proceedings and slander, and as a consequence of these facts, there is another set of publications on the subject, which saw the light of day in Greece and America. Of these publications, the reader will find a list below, in section A.2.2.3.

The second period, the settlement of loans, is extended over nearly sixty years. For reasons discussed below, during the entire reign of King Othon serious negotiations were not held between Greece and its creditors. Some sincere attempt at a settlement before the final agreement was made in the years 1827-1832, and then after the arrival of King George. Information regarding early attempts can be found in the work of Mamoukas (*Vicissitudes of the Greek Risorgimento*, 1839 - '52, 11 volumes) and Parish (*Diplomatic and financial history of Greece*, a book which we will discuss dealing with the Sixty Million Loan). As for the attempts made after the arrival of King George, Gennadios' report is an excellent document that later contributed to the achievement of the transaction (Report of 17/29 December 1875, published three years later).

Finally, the *White Paper on the conversion of the loans of 1824 and 1825* (*Λευκή Βίβλος, Μετατροπή των δανείων του 1824 και 1825*) reports in detail everything about this subject.

These is the summary of the sources available for research on the Independence Loans. In the following, we will cite some other sources that have proven useful.

A.1. Granting and use of the first loan

Many times it was observed that while the military, diplomatic, and above all political histories have countless scholars and investigators, economic history, without which all the acts of a people are left without explanation, was entirely overlooked until recent times. This observation is highly relevant in the case of the Greek Risorgimento, in relation to which large volumes of military, political and diplomatic history are never compensated even by a chapter devoted to the consideration of those events from an economic standpoint.

While our Independence War (the most important event of the nineteenth century, according to a famous article of Baron de Coubertin in the *Figaro*) was a unique event in triggering the emotional participation of the world and gave rise to a vast literature, still in study of its fortunes we continue to deepen our knowledge of the battles, the number of soldiers and ships, the names and deeds of generals, admirals, diplomats and politicians. Nonetheless, we remain ignorant of the means by which fighters were fed and ships were armed and maintained together with the central government offices, which were surely rudimentary, but not nonexistent.

This deficit is certainly explained by the difficulty of writing the economic history of an era lacking any regularly compiled budget or balance sheet, and then by the fact that in the great variety of writings on the subject of struggle for liberation, it was natural to overlook the less pleasant things and the arguments that seem insignificant at first superficial glance. One who can write of the exploits of kleftes, the successes of Kanaris at war, the fall of Missolonghi, and the armies of Ibrahim and Dramalis has to deal with matters far more attractive to himself and to his readers than the history of economics, especially since the study of this is almost impossible to accomplish on account of the scarcity of sources.

In order that the readers can get an idea of accounting that was held at the time of Independence, let us see a fragment of a report[7]

---

[7] I take these phragments from vol. 5° of Paparrigopoulos' *History*, pages 744-748, because I was unable to find the original text of the report, despite patient research. According to a scholar having authoritative knowledge of Independence, this report probably was published as a supplement of the *Geniké Efemerís*, but the supplements of that issue of the newspaper are not found in libraries.

submitted to the National Assembly on 11 April 1827 by a Commission on National Accounts which had been formed. The reports of the Commission, which was composed by Pylados, Tassikas, Pankalos, Oikonomidos and Skandalidos, indicate that the records of the national accounts were "adulterated and full of abuse, lies, omissions, errors and anomalies." Despite all of the contributions coming from people who were subjected to the levying of heavy taxes and duties, the resources were used for everything except the needs of war. At the beginning of the first period of independence, it was resolved to issue 17,250 domestic bonds, representing a capital of five million Piastres: 3,688 of these bonds were placed with a value of 1,471,000 Piastres, and another 408 corresponding to 42,100 Piastres were not located. So, the accounts lack 13,154 bonds, amounting to 3,486,900 Piastres. Still, in accounts of the second period there were 339,098 Piastres paid to various people as repayment of funds lent to the government, but there is no reference to the time of these loans or the use that was made of them. Nowhere is the indication "of the divisions and destinations of grain, ammunition and similar materials purchased in large amounts with public money by the Ministry of Economy, and distributed for public use, and there are not even records of mortgages." Moreover, "in the accounting records there are strange sales of public owned real estate, at prices that are not reasonable."

But something else indicates the most relevant data: Nowhere are recorded the values of war materials that were sent to Greece by the Committee for National Loans appointed by the government and living in London: These supplies were worth millions. Neither requisitions are recorded, nor the acts that allowed them. The auditors' report notes that "of all contributions donated to the people by Greeks and philhellenes resident inside and outside the country since the beginning of the war until the end of the third period, contributions whose total amounts to several millions of Piastres, very few passed through the registers, not more than a few hundreds of thousands of Piastres."

Of all those who wrote on the Independence, including Paparrigopoulos, only Finlay, animated by the practical spirit of his people, took care to inquire about the resources available for the war,

---

Paparrigopoulos does not quote his source.

devoting several pages to the subject[8]. Yet unfortunately we cannot give full faith even to him, because this writer, although not lying, tells just a part of the truth, with systematic and intentional omissions.

Despite the paucity of sources, I was able to reconstruct in detail at least one of the most important economic events of Independence, the one of the two debts contracted in England in 1824 and 1825 and known as Independence Loans. Although delimited, this argument is of no ordinary importance. This is the case, first of all, because there are numerous related issues deserving further study for themselves, some of which are of international law. And then, above all, it is because the granting of these loans was one of those events in which the process of restoration of our nation progressed to a more advanced stage, not less than after the recognition of Greece as a belligerent nation by the British Minister Canning in 1823. Certainly, the negotiation of the loans had even greater influence than our recognition as belligerents. So Gervinus states: "The negotiation of loans in England was more important than all the victories on the field. Everyone knew that the deepest meaning of these financial transactions was the fact that the Greek people was recognized under the protection of England, and in many circles the establishment of these economic relations was considered equivalent to the de facto recognition of the Greek state."[9] And third, finally, the issue is important because subsequently the continuing delay in recognizing the Independence Loans exercised great influence on the financial policy of the new kingdom for more than fifty years.

But let's get the facts in order.

It was two years since the flag of freedom was hoisted at Agia Laura and our persistent and ultimately victorious struggle had begun, by land and sea.

For a long time, the war was fuelled by the meagre public revenues available, through banditry and generous contributions of individuals. We can get an idea of the public revenue available from a *hypothetical budget[10]* that was discussed by the Second National Assembly at Astros. According to this document, there were

---

[8] Pages 227 and following, and 337 - 342 of his *History of the Greek Revolution*.

[9] Gervinus, Vol. 2° page 15.

[10] See Mamoukas, vol. 3°, pages 24-59.

revenues for 12,846,220 Piastres and expenses for 38,616,000, and it is notable that the document itself recognizes that it approaches the truth only on the expenditure side, because for the revenues there was no secure information, and the document was based on information gathered by representatives coming from different provinces. However, the recorded chapters of entry were the following:

Incomes from	Piastres
Crete	7,383,620
Islands	1,419,100
Eastern Greece	708,200
Western Greece	729,500
Peloponnese	2,605,800
Total	12,846,220

Tab. 1

The tax system was the Turkish one, based on oppressive taxes, and it was not possible to be otherwise. The public real estate and freshwater and marine fishing farms yielded not a little: The national olive groves of Crete alone contributed five million Piastres. The grapevine seems not to exist, it appears only in the budget of the provinces of Bostitza (now Aigion) for 30,000 Piastres, and partly in that of Missolonghi for 73,000.

Just for curiosity, this is the mirror of the revenue of the province of Attica, or of Athens, as it was stated at the time:

Tithes on wheat, barley and national lands	Piastres 72,000
Mills, factories and domestic vegetable gardens	40,000
Customs	15,000
Tithes on olives and national olive groves	175,000
Total	302,000

Tab. 2

Regarding expenditure, the general budget mentioned only the half year from May to November and divided expenses as follows:

1) *Shipping charges*. The costs of a ship amounted to 10,800 Piastres per month, rising to 13,130 with maintenance and repairs. Therefore, the national fleet of sixty ships demanded 780,000 Piastres per month, to which must be added 400,000 Piastres for ammunition, and thus the overall monthly naval spending was 1,180,100 Piastres. Also according to Palma[11], ships required an

---

[11] *Letters on Greece*, page 17.

average monthly expenditure of ten thousand Piastres each, and they were ninety or one hundred in 1825, thus giving rise to over eight million for a period of eight months he considered.

2) *Military expenditures on land.* Greece had three armies: one for the siege of fortresses (Koroni, Methoni, Patras, Corinth) and the occupation of Crete, of 18,300 men, another for the garrison in the country, with 6,050 men, and a third for the campaigns, of 26,650. In total, 51,000 men, for which 2,044,000 Piastres were spent monthly, plus another 400,000 for weapons. Thus, the commitment of naval and earth military expense reached up to 3,624,000 Piastres.

The rest of the Civil Service did not cost more than 500,000 Piastres, for a total monthly expenditure of 4,124,000, or 24,724,000 Piastres between May and November. In the winter months, spending was reduced by half, so the annual total was 38,616,000, compared to the revenue of 12,846,220 Piastres.

It is clear that we cannot pay unquestioned faith to these numbers. Nevertheless, the budget submitted to the Second National Assembly on 15 April 1823, although *hypothetical* according to the same men who wrote it, illuminates greatly the financial history of Independence. And thanks to this document we know that, even in a time when events were favourable, the revenue did not reach even one-third of the costs, even if accounts were considered in the most optimistic way. We learn from the document that over half of the revenue came from Crete, so that after the loss of the big island, all revenue at disposal of the Greek Government amounted only to five million Piastres. As counterproof, just after the loss of Crete, Gordon[12] accounted government revenues in 5,587,000 in Piastres, or 93,000 Pounds for 1825.

Then there were the contributions of individuals, mostly voluntary, and sometimes mandatory. For example, a compulsory levy was decreed by the Senate (*gerousía*) of the Peloponnese on 22 July 1822.

This is the text of the rare document[13]:

> The country in danger calls all the wealthy men to contribute to the sacred struggle for its physical, moral and political existence. Therefore, the central Government of the Peloponnese and the valiant

---

[12] *History of the Greek Revolution*, vol. 2°, page 273.

[13] The original text of the decree was published by Fotilas in the newspaper *Estía* on April 2, 1904.

A. The Independence Loans (1824-1825)

General, Mr. Theodoros Kolokotronis, have established a contribution from the said wealthy men, and send to the entire Peloponnese Messrs. Senators Andreas Kalamogdartis, Christodoulos Acholos and Karapaulos Elias, along with the noble lord Panagiotis Sofianopoulos, accompanied by the police force, and to them they confer any power necessary to force people in the list here below to pay the amounts determined for each of them, and to withdraw sums of money as may be deemed just and proportionate to the substance of each from any well-off across the province not included in the list below, and to give valid receipt until the imminent issuance of bonds of the Government in favour of lenders, to whom the Senate and General promise in the name of the nation to repay the loans received after the Restoration.

The list included among others, these names followed by the allotments:

Από την *Βοστίτζαν* ο Δ. Μελετόπουλος 10,000,

από την *Πράστα* ο Παν. και Αναγ. Τροχάνης 75,000,

από τα *Καλάβρυτα* ο Ασημάκης Φωτήλας 18,000, ο Σ. Χαραλάμπης 30,000, ο Ι. Παπαδόπουλος 60,000 και οι Ζαϊμαίοι 20,000.

Από το *Άργος* ο Χ. Περούκας 25,000.

Από τας *Πάτρας* ο Ιωάννης Παπαδιαμαντόπουλος 15,000, ο Αθανάσιος Κανακάρης 20,000, ο Ν. Λόντος 50,000, ο Π. Μπουκαούρης 10,000.

Από την *Καρύταιναν* οι αδελφοί Δεληγιανναίοι 120,000, οι αδελφοί Ταμπακόπουλοι 20,000.

Από τον *Μιστρά* ο Α. Κοπανίτζας 50,000, ο Παν. Κρεββατάς 30,000, ο Άγιος Λακεδαιμονίων 15,000, οι Αδελφοί Σαλταφέρα 10,000, ο Αναγν. Γραμματικάκης 15,000.

Από την *Αρκαδίαν* ο Πρωτοσύγγελος Αμβρόσιος 25,000, ο Γρ. Πασχάλης 20,000, ο Θ. Σκορδάκης 15,000.

Από την *Γαστούνην* ο Γ. Σισίνης 40,000, ο Ι. Σισίνης 20,000.

Από τον *Άγιον Πέτρον* ο Π. Σαρίγιαννης 25,000.

Από την *Καλαμάτα* ο Αθ. Κυριάκος 10,000.

Από το *Νησίον* οι Αδελφοί Μιχαλόπουλοι 25,000.

The decree is dated Argus, 29 July 1822, and bears the signatures and seals of the Senate of the Peloponnese and of Theodoros Kolokotronis. The newspaper article in which the decree is reproduced is of the opinion that the rich Peloponnese obeying the decision of the Senate paid the allotted amounts so that 1,066,000 Piastres were collected, although at that time the Peloponnese was in a state of near abandonment, and most of the properties were in ruins.

The systematic robbery allowed the sale of part or whole of the booty to the benefit of the community, and constituted an important source of entry during the first period of Independence. Dimitrios Ypsilantis[14] proposed to establish a rule that a given part of the loot would be paid to the public as cash, but the idea received no response except for laughter and ironic comments. After the conquest of Tripoli, where Ypsilantis could not be present, Kefalas offered him ten copper tablespoons by way of first fruits for erecting the altar of the Fatherland. Similarly, only a small part of the treasures held in the fortress of Acrocorinth was given the benefit of the government cash[15].

It was clear to everyone that such a system would not have lasted long, as government revenues were extremely limited, while the Turks that could be stripped by the brigandage migrated rapidly, and our people were impoverished every day. For all of these reasons, that unique financing system, which perhaps would be enough to feed local little fighting efforts and short impromptu raids, could not meet the continuing need for a real state fleet and planned and prolonged military campaigns. The need for foreign borrowing became more urgent every day, until the chance to contract it began to appear realistic tanks to the favourable trend of the war.

Then began two kinds of attempts to get loans: attempts of Greeks sent in search of European lenders, and attempts of brokers who came down to Greece on their own initiative. The Areopagus of Mainland Greece (Chérsos Ellas) decided to contract a debt of 150,000 florins, to be settled in five years, and entrusted the necessary negotiations to Baron Theocharis, Ch. Drosinos and Kefalas Olympios, sending the last to Europe, where he could obtain a loan of 40,000 Florins in Zurich 16 September 1823, and one of 62,000 in Marseille on 16 November of that year[16].

At the same time, Metaxas and the French Jourdain undertook negotiations for a loan of four million Francs by the Knights of Rhodes. These negotiations, about which Jourdain's book gives an account in full[17], became quite singular and can be summarized as follows: Jourdain was sent by Metaxas in Ancona, and thence to

---

[14] Not the more famous Alèxandros (Editor's note).

[15] Mendelssohn-Bartholdy, in Blachos Greek translation, vol. 1°, pages 322 and 325.

[16] See Mamoukas, vol. 1°, pages 91 – 92. Pages 93 and 94 of the same book contain two quittances of Kefalas for these loans.

[17] *Mémoires*, vol. 1°, pages 187-250 and 269-300.

Paris to begin negotiations. There, he made the acquaintance of Raoul, advocate of the Order of the Knights of St. John of Jerusalem, which, after losing Malta, was trying very hard to buy back some geographic region in which to establish itself as an independent state. The Knights showed themselves disposed to lend four million, demanding in return the sovereignty over the islands of Rhodes, Karpathos and Astipaleia, where the Order had already dwelt in other times, and before the time of taking possession and settling in these islands also requiring the temporary occupation of the island of Syros and of some deserted islands in the southwestern Peloponnese.

But since the Order neither possessed any military force nor had any credit, Jourdain found himself not only having to seek a loan of four million in the name of Greece, but also to look for another six million for the use of the Order, as we can read in the Treaty between Greece and the Order signed on 18 July 1823 by the same Jourdain[18]. A month after the signing of this treaty, the Knights sent Marquis de Saint-Croix Molay as ambassador to Greece. But the Greeks, says Trikoupis[19], took the whole affair as a joke, tore the treaty, and sent the ambassador back home. But it is right to remember that the Knights made some serious attempts to find credit, first looking for a loan of 640,000 Pounds on the London market through the banker Hullet, and then in Paris[20].

Regardless of the negotiations with the Knights of Rhodes, other contemporary negotiations were carried forward in Italy; to conduct them, Metaxas having gone back to Greece, Germanos of Patras and Mavromichalis remained in Ancona. Romas made many attempts to find a loan of one million Florins, as we can read in his nice exchanges of letters with Germanos. But unfortunately, "the divisions of the Greeks (*graikoi*) undermined the confidence of the partners of the banker" who was to grant the loan, and so the negotiations did not reach any conclusion[21].

Still, and in parallel to the action of the representatives sent to

---

[18] *Mémoires*, vol. 1°, pages 190-199.

[19] Τρικούπης, *Ιστορία της Ελληνικής Επαναστάσεως*, Vol. 3°, page 100.

[20] See *Mémoire remis à un banquier de Paris pour le déterminer à ouvrir un emprunt de 10 millions en faveur de l'ordre de Malte*, reproduced in *Mémoires* by Jourdain at pages 269-283.

[21] See letters of 16/28 February 1824 in *Αρχείον Ρώμα*, page 221.

Europe, according to the testimony of Mavrocordatos[22], the government received repeated offers of credit: 1) by a certain Roupenthal, who claimed to have relations with the banker Laffitte; 2) by Poerio, Lieutenant of General Pepe, who proposed not one but three lending projects: by the same General Pepe, by the merchant Gregory of London, and by British commander John Dogle; and 3) by a certain Robert Peacock, who arrived in Tripoli following Spiridion Korgialenios, a "well-known merchant of Kefalonia" according to Mavrocordatos, who had an important part in the war as a banker and financier in the service of Byron. Peacock was the bearer of the proposals of a Count de Wuitz, self-proclaimed "former general in the service of Russia and representative of the East India Company."

It is clear that most of these proposals were not serious. Specifically, the proposals of General Pepe were rejected by the government as inadequate, while the in the *Apology* de Wuitz and Roupenthal are qualified as mere adventurers. The first had surely meddled in the business of Cyprus loans, which we will discuss below, and is known having been judged *swindler and impostor* by an English court. The Roupenthal was found snuck in the business of Missolonghi loan[23].

However, the number of expressed proposals certifies that the idea of granting a loan to Greece had become current in Europe. There was just the need of a favourable opportunity, and this came because among the Greeks engaged in research of loan there was Andreas Louriotis, who had visited Spain and Portugal, and from there had reached London, where he became acquainted with Edward Blaquière, who presented Louriotis to the most important philhellenes London. Asked about the assumption of a loan, the London philhellenes did not discard immediately the idea, but at a meeting on 3 March 1823 they decided to send Blaquière and Louriotis back to Greece to acquire a more precise knowledge of the situation. The provisional Government of Tripoli welcomed them with enthusiasm, hoping that the deal would propitiate the progress of all Greek things, as Mavrokordatos wrote.

Indeed, the situation was deplorable. The ordinary income, which as we know barely covered a third of the costs, were very uncertain,

---

[22] *Apology*, by Orlandos and Louriotis, pages 12 - 16

[23] *Apology*, pages 194-195.

and half of them came from Crete. Finding domestic sources of extraordinary entry was impossible, and bonds issued by the government were exchanged at 15 to 17% of the nominal value. All individuals were so depleted that it was not possible to find someone who could lend eighteen dollars, which were to be used to send Praidis to Kefalonia, officially charged with welcoming Lord Byron on his arrival in Greece.

So, as soon as Louriotis disclosed the favourable inclinations of the Philhellenic Committee, the government by decree of 2 June 1823 gave to Orlandos, Louriotis and Zaímis the full power to contract a debt of four million Spanish dollars, by acting in ways that they would consider more convenient. On the 24th of that month, Mavrokordatos wrote a very clear letter to the three Commissioners giving his instructions regarding the signing of the loan and the attitude that should be taken in respect of foreign Powers, namely England[24].

Before Greece could get the loan, almost eight months passed, and this was due to continuous internal divisions, which began to manifest themselves at that time and that in November led into the first episode of civil war, and to the fact that the shortage of public financial resources had aggravated at such a sign, that the government could not find the money for the voyage to London of its three representatives. Upon leaving, they had been equipped with government letters of credit for 100,000 Piastres, payable in the Ionian islands, but upon arriving there, they did not find anybody willing to accept them. Byron had to intervene, offering the government a loan of 4,000 Pounds, and it was through this sum that the three Commissioners were able to get to London.

This slowdown, however, in some ways was propitious. First, because in the meantime Blaquière had been able to prepare the background, writing a *Report of the present state of the Greek federation* and submitting it to the Greek Committee on 23 September, a report where he painted the things of Greece in rose colour, and which was welcomed very kindly by the public opinion. And then, because in the meantime England had entered one of those periods of speculative fever that appear periodically and that propel the City people to more risky enterprises. Typically, these crises have their roots in the fall of the current interest rate, which increases the

---

[24] The decree and the letter are in *Apology*, pages 11-16.

money supply. Capitals do not find any more sufficient stable employment, and they begin to chase higher profits at the cost of reduced security, and gradually the public becomes affected by a speculative mania that ends inevitably in catastrophe. The phenomenon is so well known that it gave rise to a proverbial saying in British business circles: "John Bull can bear many things, but he cannot bear two percent," i.e., the return of the safe bonds of the British Crown.

The period of high speculation that started in mid-1823[25] had the special nature of uncontrolled inclination to lend to foreign governments, and even to governments that had not yet been officially recognized, such as Brazil, Chile, Colombia and others. Here is a list of loans in those years in London, in Pounds:

Year	Country	Nominal Capital	Price %
1822	Chile	1.000.000	70
	Colombia	2.000.000	84
	Denmark	2.000.000	77 ½
	Peru	450.000	88
	Russia	3.500.000	81
1823	Austria	1.500.000	82
	Portugal	1.500.000	87
1824	Brazil	1.686.000	75
	Argentina	1.500.000	85
	Colombia	4.750.000	88 ½
	Greece	800.000	59
	Mexico	3.200.000	58
	Kingdom of Naples	2.500.000	91 ½
	Peru	750.000	82
1825	Brazil	4.000.000	85
	Denmark	3.500.000	75
	Greece	2.000.000	56 ½
	Guatemala	167.000	73
	Mexico	3.200.000	89 ½
	Peru	616.000	78

Tab. 3

The expression "price" here and below indicates the actual result of the placement of the bonds by private underwriters, at auction: In the case of

---

[25] That I described extensively in vol. 4th of my *History of the Bank of England*, pages 5 – 16.

Chile, in this table, it means that private investors were willing to pay 70 Pounds for a bond that represented £ 100 at maturity, and therefore the Government of Chile in fact received £ 700,000 cash in return for the commitment of one million.

And so the credit application made by a people whose recent feats shone of glory, and which, moreover, enjoyed the incomparable prestige of its antiquity, easily got full satisfaction: The first loan requested by the Greek Government was granted on 21 February, i.e., just 25 days after the arrival in London of the Greek Commissioners[26]. In the climate of enthusiasm for the Greek cause and of speculative fever, in England were found private investors willing to give credit to the Greek provinces, some of which are still unredeemed (such as Cyprus, Epirus, etc..), and to accept the reimbursement of loans after the liberation.

The signing of the loan took place on better terms than those provided by the Mavrokordatos' instructions, which prescribed: 1) that the required capital of four million dollars could be reduced even to one only, 2) that the amortization happen between ten and twenty years, 3) that the interest was of 6 - 8%. The Commissioners were able to obtain: 1) capital of £ 800,000[27], i.e. the full satisfaction of the request, 2) duration of the loan of 36 years with extinction via amortization, and amortization rate of 1%, 3) 5% interest. Very convenient conditions were obtained also for the brokers' commission (3%) and the insurance premium, set at 1 ½ percent because Greece was everywhere in a state of war: very favourable conditions, similar to those obtained years later, after peace treatises, when the Sixty Million loan was contracted with the three Powers. Finally, the loan was placed by underwriters at price of 59% of the nominal capital, i.e. approximately to the conditions provided for by the Greek Government: "Do not accept a price much lower than 60%," Mavrokordatos had written.

All government revenues were given as guarantee for the payment of interest, and all land public property as capital guarantee[28]. From

---

[26] Who got there nine days after Maitland's death, as Koresios observes.

[27] Remember that four million *dollars* or *Piastres* were equivalent to about as many French *écu*, and so to twenty million francs and 800.000 Pounds (Editor's note).

[28] See the circular letter of the *Committee of Greek Bondholders* of

the capital would be held at once the amounts necessary to guarantee the payment of the interest for the first two years.

So much about the award of our first loan; let us now examine the events surrounding the sending of money to Greece, and of the use that was made of it.

The loan, granted by bankers Loughman, O'Brien, Ellice and Company, was granted at a price of 59%, so the amount actually paid by the underwriters would be £ 472,000. But from these were subtracted 80,000 Pounds for two years of interest, 16,000 for two years of amortization, and even 3,200 Pounds for commission of 0.4% on interest. More, the 3% commission on capital was deduced[29]; so the total deductions reached up to 123,200 Pounds, and the sum actually paid was to amount to 348,800 Pounds.

The effective interest rate, with annual capitalization and including amortization, was 10.86%. In fact, the Greeks received a net sum of 348,800 Pounds, and in exchange for this, they had to pay 34 annual instalments of 48,000 Pounds beginning from the third year. At the end the loan would be repaid, because the contract included an annual fee of 1% amortization. Applying the method of determining the effective rate mortgage, we find that the rate at which the debt is zero Pounds after 34 rate is exactly 10,86092509%. For the proof, see the first loan amortization table in the Appendix.

The amount was of not little account, and then the Greek Committee, which had assumed the moral responsibility of the loan, also assumed that of sending the money and began to take precautions so that the money that cost so much effort could arrive to its destination, since in Greece everything was a mess. To understand the problem of sending the money, there is a hint in a letter that the Greek A. M. Antonopoulos living in Trieste had received from London:

London, 17 February 1824

The loan of the Greeks (*graikoi*) ended at 59% in a respectable[30] house ... the Greeks should be grateful to the Committee and especially to the

---

7 November 1862, published in a booklet.

[29] Andreadis here must have neglected to correct carefully the text in galleys, because the text does not mention the commission, yet it indicates £ 123,000 (not 123,200, more correctly) as the total of the deductions, but £ 348,800 as the sum actually paid. (Editor's note).

[30] *Respectable,* in the text *rispettabile,* in Italian. The "respectable" house was the London Mansion House, according to Cochrane, vol.

tireless Bowring. The Committee and the Government Representatives[31] agreed to send the money to Lord Byron and Colonel Stanhope, and let them deliver it to the Parliament preventing thieves seizing it.[32]

It was agreed, therefore, that the money would be sent to Zakynthos, to Kaisar Logothetis, a citizen of that island, and to the English merchant Samuel Barff, who was also residing there, and that it would not be delivered to the Greek Government without the express consent of Byron, Colonel Stanhope and Lazaros Koundouriotis. The decision gave rise to new delays, because Byron, whose consent was necessary, had died, and so new instructions from London were requested. These delays caused the British representative[33] to threaten leaving from the Ionian Islands, but then came the new instructions, and 308,000 Pounds in cash and 11,900 in ammunition were handed over to the Greek Government, the remaining £ 28,100 having been kept in London[34].

Delivered to Greece through these vicissitudes, the 308,000 Pounds, like the money of the next second loan, were not invested in the cause of freedom, but in that of the struggle for hegemony and supremacy over rivals. The loans themselves became responsible for a great deal of civil conflict: The political responsibility appeared far more palatable when it involved the availability of substantial capital. As also noted Palma[35], a determining ground of the Civil War was the fact that the government did not give account for the money of the loans.

2, page 368 (Editor's note).

[31] *Deputati* in Italian in the text (Editor's note).

[32] *Αρχείον Ρώμα*, page 227-228.

[33] See Mendelssohn-Bartholdy, ib., page 457 and the extended reports about the story in *Narrative of a Second visit to Greece* by Blaquière, pages 5 and 14. Blaquière is a particularly important witness because he was the bearer of money into Greece, and on the subject he held a correspondence with the Mavrokordatos, partly reproduced in the book, which contains also the known story of the last days of Byron.

[34] The total lacks £ 800, probably due to another misprint (Editor's note).

[35] *Letters on Greece*, page 7.

The misuse of British money is attested by almost all historians[36]. The ambassador in Constantinople wrote: "The benefits of the loan has been confined to the navy and the neighborhood of Napoli of Romania[37]. Those who have not touched the dollars are disgusted at the manner of their expenditure."[38] Finlay writes about this with great detail and with visible malice; according to him, the members of the government spent money with *dishonesty as well as extravagance*, the greatest military leaders allowed themselves to be bribed to attack their own countrymen, and members of the legislature squandered not small sums for the salaries of their many useless political acolytes, pompously named public officials. Our historians and the most favorable to us among foreign historians refrain from dealing with this issue. Only one of them takes up the defense of the Greek Government: the chivalrous and philhellene Count Palma, a Spanish nobleman relentless in the battle for the Greek cause in England, who insists on writing that the money was spent for the fleet and that there was no waste. In his own way, in addition to Bulwer, Finlay also confirms that the money was spent on the fleet, stating that "the waste of money on the navy was even greater than on the army."

Finlay's book contains seven pages[39] of testimony corroborating his allegations, but when it comes time to speak of the squandering of the second loan by the British and Americans, he gets along with three rows. Among the evidence cited, there are some bright and soaked-in-bitter-truth pages that he himself had written as a correspondent for *The Times* in Athens. More interesting than anything else is when he describes the craze (which affected everybody) of glittering uniforms imported from Thessaloniki and Ioannina at significant expense. It seems that this mania has infected even the professionals and Phanariots in frock coats who had

---

[36] See Mendelssohn-Bartholdy, ib. pp 457 - 458. — Bulver - (H. L.) *An autumn in Greece*, pages 14 - 17. — *Renseignements sur la Grèce et l'administration du Comte Capodistrias* (Par un témoin oculaire des faits qu'il rapporte), pages 118 - 123. The author of this document, Biàros Kapodistrias, furious against Kondouriotis, considered him mainly responsible for the squandering of money.

[37] Understand Nauplia (Editor's note).

[38] Bulver, page 20.

[39] Finlay, vol. 2°, from page 34 forward.

immigrated into Nauplia, of whom Finlay gives us this picture full of life[40]:

> Every man of any consideration in his own imagination wanted to place himself at the head of a band of armed men, and hundreds of civilians paraded the streets of Nauplia with trains of kilted followers, like Scottish chieftains. Phanariots and doctors in medicine, who, in the month of April 1824 were clad in ragged coats, and who lived on scanty rations, threw off that patriotic chrysalis before summer was past, and emerged in all the splendour of brigand life, fluttering about in rich Albanian habiliments, refulgent with brilliant and unused arms, and followed by diminutive pipe-bearers and tall henchmen. The small stature, voluble tongues, turnspit legs, and Hebrew physiognomies of these Byzantine emigrants, excited the contempt, as much as their sudden and superfluous splendour awakened the envy, of the native Hellenes. Nauplia certainly offered a splendid spectacle to any one who could forget that it was the capital of an impoverished nation struggling through starvation to establish its liberty. The streets were for many months crowded with thousands of gallant young men in picturesque dresses and richly ornamented arms, who ought to have been on the frontiers of Greece.

Judging from the attitude of Finlay, German Gervinus notes that "Finlay, describing in detail the manner in which the Greek Government squandered the loans, was pleased to dwell in a series of accusations none of which strictly speaking was false, but that are however targeting poor people, kleftès and people confused by the sudden availability of a wealth, much less dishonest than proved to be some peoples among the richest and most civilized, who robbed those thieves right in the most dramatic moment for them."[41] And studying the events of the second loan, we shall see how appropriate this observation of Gervinus was.

Readers might oppose to me that I am not capable of anything else but comparing the opinions of foreign writers in relation to this important topic. But it is precisely through the comparison of discordant opinions of Finlay and Gervinus that I express the judgment that I can give of the problem: I blame like Finlay the corruption and stupidity of politicians and military commanders at the time, but I think that they cannot be judged without taking into account the conditions in which they lived at the time of Independence. In all cases, the guilt of these men cannot be judged

---

[40] Finlay, vol. 2°, page 39.

[41] Gervinus, vol. 2°, pages 129-133 of the Greek translation.

A. The Independence Loans (1824-1825)

more harshly than those of bankers in London and New York.

A.2. *Granting and use of the second loan*

The successful conclusion of the first loan and the increased need for extra revenues for Greece persuaded the Commissioners that it was possible and necessary to find a second one, and an amount greater than the first. This idea, which began to be discussed on 27 March 1824, gave rise to some conflict inside the government and the Parliament[42], who both feared the danger of imminent attack from Egypt without being able to take appropriate measures to face it. Finally, the Parliament rushed to vote for the signing of a loan of 15 million dollars on 31 July 1824, and the government, namely the Executive, as it was said then, on 14 August charged Orlandos, Louriotis and Zaimis to negotiate the loan in the ways they would consider possible.

The Commission, however, changed in composition. Ioannis Zaimis, recognized by Finlay to be an able and honest man, remained in the Commission only a short time, and in fact he had already been excluded on 12 February, because his relatives were partisans of the faction that was hostile to the government. Some months later, he was replaced by Spaniolakis, "whose appointment," wrote the executive to the other two Commissioners, "was made for the sake of appearances, and is only meant to bring you information on the situation at home, and to deliver a letter to Mr. Canning."[43] But Spaniolakis, man of many virtues and later Minister of Economy, did not limit himself to appearances and wanted to be involved in the affairs of the loan. That's because from that moment on, the decisions concerning the loan fell upon the shoulders of Orlandos and Louriotis, and yet we find always objections by Spaniolakis to their acts. Being a man of difficult character, he got into conflict with the other two Commissioners, and from this conflict later arose the action against Louriotis and Orlandos before the Court of Auditors, as well as the aforementioned memory of Spaniolakis against the *Apology*.

The two Commissioners left immediately to contract the new loan in Paris and London, and were well received in both markets. After lengthy discussions, the proposals of the London bankers were the preferred choice, offering 50 million Francs, while the availability of the French never exceeded ten million guaranteed (*fermées*) and

---

[42] See *Apology*, vol. 1° pages 22-24.

[43] See *Apology*, vol. 2°, page 35.

another ten to be paid if needed (*facultatifs*). According to the proposal of the French bankers, the loan would be granted by the two banks André & Cottier and André Odier & Ce. The price was 59%, interest 5% and amortization 1% of the nominal capital. The sum given was reduced by one million for the interest of the first two years, and then by 500,000 Francs for commission and 550,000 for amortization and other expenses. So, deducting 2,050,000 Francs to 59% of the nominal capital, 3,850,000 Francs would be delivered[44]. There was no way to connect the French proposal with the English one, because English bankers demanded exclusivity from the beginning.

The London loan was borrowed by the bank of the brothers Ricardo. It consisted of a nominal capital of £ 2 million, divided into 200,000 bonds at 10 Pounds each[45]. The bonds were offered on the market at 55 and ½ of the nominal value, returning a yield of 1,100,000 Pounds, from which you had to subtract:

1	Interest of the first two years	200,000
2	Amortization if the first year 1%	20,000
3	2% commission on interest	4,000
4	Commission, brokerage and charges 3% one off	60,000
	Total	*284,000*

Tab. 4

The amount which remained to be paid in cash was 816,000 Pounds. The anticipation of the first two years of interest to creditors, together with the continuing climate of speculation and stability of the listing of bonds of the first loan that lasted during the subscription for the second (they were exchanged on the stock market to 60% of the nominal value, i.e., 4½% more than the new loan, a fact however that did not allow that the second loan would be issued at this best price, although some believed it possible, including Spaniolakis), ensured that the placement of the second loan was very successful, collecting subscriptions for more than twice the capital offered. "The influx of bidders was so plentiful," says Spaniolakis[46], "that made their sum after two days the subscriptions

---

[44] The text of the contract, with date 5 February 1825, is at page 127-129 of *Apology*, vol. 2°.

[45] Or perhaps 20.000 at £ 100 each: the text gives 200.000 at 100, with evident misprint (Editor's note).

[46] *Observations on the Apology of Orlandos and Louriotis*, page 40.

were found amounting to four and a half million, instead of the two forecast. Messrs. Ricardo, not to displease anyone, assigned to each bidder the proportionate part of the offer made."

The placement of the bonds was then a splendid success, but the result of the deal once again ended in a catastrophe. The two Commissioners — of which Gervinus wrote that one, Louriotis, was a man of good intentions but of little value, and the other, Orlandos, was honest but extremely stubborn — this time had been able to get the loan without needs of the Greek Committee, and therefore they decided to escape the harsh, but in many ways useful, control of the philhellenes of the Committee. Thus, they deprived themselves of the watchfulness of men who, taking responsibility for the operation, considered their moral duty to take every care to ensure that the loan was spent for the purpose for which it was contracted. By withdrawing themselves from the protection of the Philhellenic Committee, Orlandos and Louriotis were not really able to act independently as they hoped: Having stumbled into a world about which they did not know anything, they soon felt again the need to get help, and soon they found available the lenders Ricardo and their friends Ellice, Hobhouse and Burdett, who soon found themselves gathered in what *The Times* always called *the Tetrarchy* (well qualified as such for the first time by Earl Palma): The four bankers were transformed into omnipotent guardians, disposed of the money lent to Greece at their will and easily neglected to consult the representatives of Greece regarding decisions concerning them.

Then began the orders to ship builders to unreasonable conditions, the hiring of celebrated generals and admirals, the massive buybacks of bonds of the just-contracted loan on the Stock Exchange, without the slightest concern to send either the money or ships purchased with that money to Greece, which had been devastated by war. And although they had set contract terms for the construction and launching of the ships, the lack of penalties made all the clauses theoretical, and if we add that the contract for the construction of ships was awarded in part to unscrupulous Americans, and in part to a man in close contact with Mehmet Ali, the contractual guarantees were not theoretical, but simply ridiculous.

The Times, to which mainly is due the discovery of the orgiastic squandering of the loan through a long series of articles in the fall of

1826[47], wrote in an article of 26 October that "the Greek loan followed the fate of the man going from Jerusalem to Jericho who met the robbers, but this time he did not find the good Samaritan ... Greece has lost all the benefits of the loan. The Greek cause was betrayed, and this happened just in England, and it would triumph today if it were not for England and the British stock market." The waste of the money that was made in England attracted the attention of philhellenes from all over the world. The banker Eynard wrote to Stanhope that the very first duty of the Philhellenic Committee of London was now to obtain a statement of the use of the loan because the mismanagement of the loan in England was leading Greece to the brink of disaster, but then it was Greece that was considered responsible for the waste[48]. Stanhope, meanwhile, had convened a joint meeting of philhellenes and investors in the bonds: The meeting was held in the City of London Tavern on 5 September 1826, and had appointed a committee to clear up the matter. The report of this commission, presented on 23 October, said, among other things, that "while Messrs. O'Brien and Loughman and the representatives of Greece provided the Commission with any requested information, Messrs. Ricardo not only refused to recognize the Commission, but tried to interpose any obstacle to the establishment of truth too." [49]

We would have the right to show even more severity toward the abuses that occurred in England, if the use of the little money which came to Greece did not lead us to the painful conclusion that the Greek cause would be betrayed even without the intrusion of English speculators. To betray the Greek cause was more than enough the mentality of many of our patriots of that time, willing to sacrifice everything else, but not to give up the feelings of party. Thus, with British speculators on one side and Greece torn by internal conflict on the other, the power to decide on the use of loans had fallen entirely on two individuals, Orlandos and Louriotis, who were in

---

[47] Issues of 5, 12, 20, 27 September, 23, 24, 26, 27, 28, 31 October, 1, 3, 4 and 13 November. The articles were collected by Gennadios in his essay *The Greek Loans*, etc.

[48] Letter published by *The Times* of 27 September.

[49] The report can be read entirely in *The Times* of 24 October. In the issue of 20 September, there is a letter by Ricardo, and other articles are in the issues of 25 – 30 October, among which is one by Louriotis with the title *A Voice from Marathon*.

London with an ill-defined role and an exaggerated responsibility on their shoulders. According to Gervinus, the two "were brave, but also arrogant. Concerned about the situation they were living, missing well defined instruction, likely to receive conflicting advice, discordant the one with the other, sometimes suspicious and wary with friends, sometimes careless and confident of their enemies, helpless in a world market such as London, completely unaware of what were the stock-jobbers in the city, they were not able to cope with the cunning of the insolent British bankers."[50]

But here are the details of the use of the second debt.

Issued at 55 ½%, it put at disposal of the two Commissioners the sum of 1,100,000 Pounds, to which were to be added £ 18,100[51] remaining from the first loan, plus 2,200 from a collection of the Greek community of Calcutta, at that time flourishing and committed from the beginning to the cause of Independence, and even 10,500 Pounds of interest on bonds of the first and second loan repurchased on the Stock Exchange.

So, the Greek Government had 1,150,800 Pounds actually available in London, or 28,770,000 Francs, an incredible sum for a government not recognized, and in constant danger of ceasing to exist. The sum was consumed in three main chapters:

1) money spent on the London Stock Exchange for the issuance, service, and the extinction of debts: Around 496,200 Pounds, it is nearly half of the total.

2) money spent in England and the United States for military and naval supplies: 392,600 Pounds from which Greece obtained almost no benefit.

3) money paid in cash to the Greek Government, which spent it on purchases, 232,558 Pounds.

The total is 1,121,778 Pounds, with an extra 28,880[52] that were used to cover the expenses of the Commissioners and other various needs.

---

[50] Vol. 2°, pages 15-18 and 127-133.

[51] The previous chapter talks of £ 28.100. We have seen that the text contains numerous misprints in figures (Editor's note).

[52] Really, 29.022, as is understood in the following § A.2.3 (Editor's note).

A.2.1. Money spent in the London Stock Exchange

Under this title are computed 20,000 Pounds as interest of the first two years of the loan, and 64,000 in fees owed to the Ricardos (3% on the nominal capital and 2% on interest). These were items of the contract, similar to those of the first loan, and to which there is no objection. The commission paid to the Ricardos is not to be considered excessive, though perhaps it could be limited to two percent, and at the time had caused severe objections: "Messrs. Ricardo have pocketed 64,000 Pounds," says *The Times* of 5 September 1826. Ten days earlier, the same newspaper had examined the action of the Philhellenic Committee of Paris and had reported that contributions in 1825 amounted to 239,649 Francs, while those in the first half of 1826 had risen to 651,867, and included donations from Eynard for 25,000 Francs, from the family of the Dukes of Orleans and the future Louis-Philippe for 27,000, from Casimir Perrier for 6,000 and many others, plus 129,881 Francs collected door-to-door in Paris. However, the English newspaper lamented, what are these figures against the profits of the loans used in a careless and immoral way in England? Coming to the Ricardos, *The Times* added: "The pretty item reserved as commission by the contractors of the second loan (amounting to £ 64,000) nearly doubles the voluntary contributions of all the Philhellenes in Europe, including those of committees and corporations, of colleges and universities, of classical ladies and benevolent princes — of priests, artists, philosophers and statesmen — the produce of benefit concerts, and the collection of charity sermons."

But another 212,220 Pounds in London were used in the repurchase of bonds, and the judgment on this point must be severe. The buyback was partly a result of contractual conditions, in part a consequence of the mere will of the Tetrarchy. According to the agreement of the second loan, Greece had to buy back bonds of the first one for £ 250,000 at face value in order to push the Greek bonds revaluation on the stock market and to strengthen the credit of the Greek Government. So, £ 250,000 worth of bonds were bought at the current rate, thereby spending £ 113,200.

It is obvious that this operation was advantageous only from an abstract point of view. First, because at the time of the agreements for the second loan the bonds of the first were listed at sixty percent[53]

---

[53] Rates from December 1824 to February 1825 can be read in

of face value, and therefore it was genuine insanity to issue new bonds at 55½% and use them to buy back the older ones (after a short time, they were lowered quickly in correspondence with the unfortunate events at the homeland: On 4 October 1825, they were lowered by 24-25%, and on 27 October by 30%[54]). Secondly, because this was by no means necessary to the success of the second loan, for which all other benefits it envisaged to subscribers were sufficient. Third and most important reason, because Greece was in need of immediate relief, and could very well leave after the liberation all concerns about the extinction of its debt. And then we just have to recognize that the buyback of these bonds was inserted in the contract for the sole purpose of providing the opportunity to earn more commissions to the brokers Ricardo.

The scandal grew larger when the Tetrarchy subtracted the management of the loan from the fragile hands of the Greek representatives and decided on the repurchases of bonds, not provided for in the contract, allocating for this purpose 99,020 Pounds, with which bonds were redeemed for 218,000 Pounds nominal value. Bonds for 91,110 Pounds were repurchased from the bankers[55] who held them. A small amount of 7,910 Pounds was used by Orlandos and Louriotis the repurchase of 14,000 Pounds nominal on the market on behalf of the government, with the intention of taking advantage of the subsequent improvement of the market, and in fact they were sold for 10,060 Pounds in 1830, the moment of the proclamation of the independence of Belgium and of King Leopold. The operation was branded as useless speculation by Spaniolakis[56],

---

Spaniolakis, Annex 7°.

[54] Documents in *Archives of Dionysios Romas*, pages 707 and 727.

[55] For precision:

- £ 158.000 nominal by the Ricardo for £ 67.895
- Another £ 8.000 and 5.000 nominal by the same Ricardo on 15 October and 19 November at 55 ½ and 56 ½ for total £ 7.265
- 25.000 nominal by Rallis for £ 11.550
- 8.000 nominal by Rallis on 12 October at 55 for £ 4.000

In total, 91.110 Pounds.

[56] Who calls into the question Maniakis, Rallis and Lee, as well. See *Observations on the Apology of Orlandos and Louriotis*, page 43.

and although after eight decades it is difficult to judge, it is certain that for Greece it would be more useful to have 7,910 Pounds available in 1826 than 10,060 four years later.

The justification for the purchases was that they would help contain the decline of Greek bonds. But since the decline was due to poor performance in the war in Greece, and not to the abundance of its bonds on the market, it was totally unreasonable to think of remedying the evil depriving Greece of the only means by which it could avoid defeat. The justification was unfounded, and was in bad faith. What was wanted was to collect commissions, and at the same time to stimulate the rise of other bonds that were in the hands of the Ricardos and their friends. The Ricardos wrote the following letter to Orlandos and Louriotis[57] with a French courtly style that leaves no doubt about the interpretation, however:

Messieurs,

Our stock exchange is now in a terrible condition: the Greek loan is listed with 10 or 11 percent discount, and there is great fear. We do not know if there is bad news, but everybody wants to sell. If you have any confidence in the affairs of Greece, and in the beautiful care that the cause deserves, would it not be in the interest of your Government to support a little the credit of Greece, and to purchase a good portion

---

[57] *Apology*, vol. 2°, page 28. The French text of the letter is following:

Messieurs,

Notre Bourse est aujourd'hui dans une condition affreuse: l'emprunt grec est à 10 et a 11 d'escompte, et il y a une peur terrible. Nous ne savons pas s'il y a de mauvaises nouvelles, mais tout le monde veut vendre. Si vous avez toute cette confiance dans les affaires de la Grèce, que ce que vous dites de la belle position de la cause mérite, ne sera-t-il pas de l'intérêt de votre Gouvernement et pour soutenir un peu son crédit, qu'une bonne portion de l' emprunt serait achetée pour son compte, d'être revendue dans un temps plus heureux? Considérez bien cette proposition. Nous et nos amis ont[57] déjà une forte quantité sur le dos, sur laquelle il y a une grande perte. Nous ne désirons pas qu'aucune chose soit faite pour nous, mais c'est désespérant de voir l'affaire dans un si mauvais état.

Votre réponse par le porteur nous obligera.

Avec considération,

Vos serviteurs dévoués Jacob et Samson Ricardo
28 Mai 1825.

of the loan on its behalf, to be sold in a happier time? Consider this proposition. We and our friends have a large amount of bonds on our shoulders, on which there is a great loss. We do not want anything to be done for us, but it is disheartening to see the matter in such a bad state.

Your answer through the bearer will oblige us.

With consideration,

Your trusty servants Jacob and Samson Ricardo

28 May 1825

Damaged by the fall of the bonds, the bankers tried to stimulate artificially their increase in value, and not succeeding, they arrived to the point of buying back some quantities at three times the current rate. This really seems like an exaggeration, but the accounts presented by the Ricardos to Spaniolakis show absolutely clearly that on 15 and 19 November 1825, the Ricardos bought bonds for 7265 Pounds rated at 55 ½ and 56 ½, and that on 12 October Rallis had bought for 8,000 rated to 55. At that moment, the market value of bonds floated between 15 and 20.

The Times article of 28 October wrote about the attitude of the British philhellenes toward the Tetrarchy. Among other stories, it tells of a Mr. Hume, who had bought 10,000 Pounds of bonds, and who ascertained the drop claimed to be compensated by the Commission, "so that Greece will not lose a great friend."[58] Another distinguished philellene was Mr. Bowring, according to *The Times*. He had subscribed £ 25,000, and after the fall, "he made vehement remonstrances coupled with representations of his services to the Greek cause," being able to have bonds bought back at a discount of 10%. But when the titles retrieved their initial listing, Bowring was able to overcome the audacity of Hume, claiming the restitution. It was pointed out that his bonds were repurchased by the Greek Government by his express request; he protested that he remembered nothing, and insisted until the Commissioners paid him other 2,500 Pounds, fully recovering the loss. *The Times* reported that this second great friend of Greece had won an £ 11,000 commission in connection with the issue of the first loan.

---

[58] About this Hume, see also *The Times* of 4 November and *Oriental Herald* of January 1826, "The Greek Loan and Mr. Hume," pages 76-80.

A.2.2. Sums spent on military and nautical equipment

This expenditure item is divided into three sections, for a total of 392,600 Pounds:

1) Supply of weapons, ammunition and guns, 77,000 Pounds;

2) Construction of ships in England and organization of mercenary troops by Cochrane, 160,000 Pounds;

3) Construction of frigates in America, 155,600 Pounds.

A.2.2.1. Supply of weapons, ammunition and guns

On this point there is little to say, unlike the next two ones. 57,000 Pounds were spent on weapons and ammunition, and 20,000 on guns. The supply of arms in England took place mainly at the workshops Burton (£ 12,206), Mackintosh (£ 10,266) and Graham (£ 26,688), and in that respect, there is not much to tell except that the two Commissioners were then charged with not being able to obtain a discount of 10% that used to be yielded to those who paid cash[59].

The purchase of the guns was ordered by the government, which wanted to strengthen fortifications and to renew the equipment of the fleet then in existence. Iron guns were ordered to replace the bronze ones of the fortress of Nauplia and others, as well as eighty pairs of iron guns for ships[60]. The Commission was able to complete only the provision of naval guns, but some failed to arrive in Greece. As for the guns of Nauplia, the Commission[61] decided to scll thc old ones made of bronze to the company Kontostavlos & C. while ordering the delivery of iron ones to Graham, but neglected to consider that the two events would not be simultaneous. When the Kontostavlos officers arrived to pick up the bronze cannons, there were still eight months to wait for the arrival of the new ones, and then, being impossible to disarm Nauplia, the government paid the penalty of £ 600, provided by the contract of sale. Later, the Court of Auditors sentenced the Commission to a fine of £ 1000 for this.

---

[59] *Apology*, pages 130 – 156 and Spaniolakis, pages 14-17.

[60] Detailed instructions by the government in *Apology*, page 54.

[61] *Apology*, page 60. A letter written by the Commission to the Government on 4 October 1825 explains the reasons of the mishandling.

A.2.2.2. *Construction of steamships in England and encroachment of Cochrane*

The need to have some steam warship was realized since the early moments of the war. Everyone acknowledged that Greece would not be able to arm a fleet comparable to that of the Sultan, mainly for financial reasons, and therefore it would be well that the quality of ships replaced the numeric inferiority. Some steamships armed with 64-litre guns would balance out the situation, being able to attack the Ottoman ships which could not move due to a lack of wind, to cut the communications of the Turks and aid manoeuvring of the incendiary boats.

The need for a steam fleet was examined in a long report to Byron in 1823[62] by Frank Abney Hastings, the heroic commander of the *Karteria*. And, realizing that for the project of Hastings there was no other obstacle than the financial one, immediately after the granting of loans, the government and the Commission set to work seriously to build a steam flotilla. But it was this affair more than any other which showed the harmful influence of the Tetrarchy, which turned what looked like an opportunity into a shameful defeat.

As soon as the constitution of the new fleet was decided upon, even before the negotiations for the second debt, Ellice, a member of the Tetrarchy and famed philellene, proposed to undertake for £ 10,000 the task of building and equipping a steam corvette of 400 tons, which was to take the name of *Karteria* and obey the command of Hastings. The proposal was accepted, and having just completed the second loan, Ellice started building the Karteria in Galloway's shipyard, and made a commitment to complete the ship with everything necessary by August 1825. But Ellice did not care to mention the penalties in the contract, so the shipyard allowed itself endless delays[63], and the Karteria arrived in Greece only in September 1826, after many vicissitudes, including a failure when it was launched. The ship did not arrive in good condition, and proved to be of minimal utility, despite the value of his commander. The above-cited article of *The Times* of 28 October 1826 notes that the fee due to Ellice was paid on 25 March 1825, fifteen months before

---

[62] Reproduced in Annex in the *History of the Greek Revolution* by Finlay.

[63] See regarding this a letter by Hastings of 16 January 1826, reproduced in *Apology*, pages 292-293.

the launching of the ship, so that "the disinterested philellene Mr. Ellice benefited from 15 months of interest."

But the events of Karteria are puny in comparison with the other supplies. Shortly after the granting of the loan, the Tetrarchy ordered five more steamships for £ 110,000, without even consulting the two Greek representatives, who wrote a letter to the Ricardos, of which there is a fragment: "You have ordered the construction of five ships, rather than buy them ready, without our permission and without even notify us."[64]

Certainly, the choice of ships ready to buy would be more responsible, since the sending of the fleet was so urgent - it was hoped to use it to cut off communications between Ibrahim Pasha and Egypt, and to block supplies for the Egyptian army short of ammunition - and since there was no certainty that the ships were completed in the allotted time. This was noticed by *The Times*, which gave notice on 12 September of the sale of an excellent steamer, Valencia, for 11,000 Pounds in those days. The tetrarchs justified themselves by saying that the ships available were not suitable to be armed with 64-litre guns. Moreover, apart from the absence of penalties in the contract, Galloway was not the right person in whom trust was placed, because he had a son in the service of Mehmet Ali, the sovereign against whom he built the ships[65].

But the construction of five ships was finally decided, and soon afterward arrived in England a certain Cochrane, who had a reputation for having done wonders in South America and was recently fired from the service of the Government of Brazil as a result of disagreements. The Tetrarchy thought to put him in command of the steam fleet, and Ellice made many promises to the Greek delegation, claiming that "within a few weeks Cochrane would be in Constantinople, ready to burn the Turkish fleet in the Golden Horn" and that "with 150,000 Pounds available, Cochrane will scour Greece from the Turks." The Commission was persuaded to sign a contract that appointed Cochrane "Admiral of the mercenary fleet," with a fee of 37,000 Pounds and with vast Powers, including the right to choose for himself the officers and sailors to whom the Greek Government would give salary and ammunition. As to the fee, it was justified as compensation for a sum of 55,000

---

[64] The text does not quote the source (Editor's note).

[65] See *The Times* of 12 September and Gervinos, ib.

Pounds, of which Cochrane was creditor from Brazil, and which he was going to lose on account of the new commitments. Still, according to the pacts, Cochrane would be entitled to part of the spoils of war[66].

The engagement of Cochrane, believed harbinger of certain triumph, helped to make sterile the expense of 113,000 Pounds for the five ships, so that adding the compensation of Cochrane, the amount spent in vain for British naval supplies reaches 150,000 Pounds, without including £ 10,000 of Karteria.

A good sailor, Cochrane was weak enough to consider himself also a great inventor, and convinced Hobhouse, Ricardo, Burdett and Ellice to experiment with a new type of steam engine of his invention on the five ships — an idea that would all the more be disregarded, since the application of the new type of engine also assumed significant modifications of the hulls of the ships, already partly built. So, the steam flotilla, an extreme source of hope for Greece, was considered by the bankers of London to be the appropriate occasion to test a prototype, and the manufacturers were ordered to change ships and equipment according to the design of Cochrane.

The outcome of the experiments is known to all those who have read something about Greek Independence. Kapodistrias was informed by Spaniolakis when he arrived in London in 1827[67]. The construction of five steamers, two major and three smaller ones, was ordered, and the vessels had to be ready in five months. One of the great ones, the *Enterprise* (*Epicheiresis*), came to be launched in London, but just out of the Thames it did not keep the sea and was about to sink. It was saved by a miracle by the British warship *Columbine*, and towed to Plymouth, where it remained nearly two months in the yard. Reinforced in the shell and featured with a modified steering, it managed to sail and reach Greece in September of 1828, where it remained unused. The other big ship, the *Invincible* (*Akatamachetos*), caught fire in the Thames during the tests.

Only one of three small ones, the Hermes, arrived in Greece under the command of Cochrane[68], and only after changing the engines.

---

[66] See the text of the contract in the *Apology*, pages 288-289.

[67] See report by Spaniolakis, Annex 8° of his book.

[68] Who had been in Greece for the first time as commander of the ship *Soter*, bought in Marseille by Eunardos and by the philhellenic Committee in Paris.

The other two were not able to navigate and rotted, mooring near London.

This is the story of the British naval supplies. Perhaps the best use of 160,000 Pounds squandered would change the fate of the war in 1826, and still more so if to the British scandal the American one had not been added.

A.2.2.3. Construction of frigates in America and Mission of Kontostavlos

The knowledge of this curious affair was made possible by the records of judicial actions moved in bad faith by American manufacturers against the Greek representative in the United States, the valuable and unfortunate Alexandros Kontostavlos, who was the victim of slander on all sides. The American causes gave occasion to numerous writings, which are collected in a series of volumes of the British Museum dedicated to the relations between the Greek Independence and the United States.

This collection contains studies, speeches, and accounts of collections of money offers, reports, etc., and would prove very useful to anyone wishing to write a history of Philhellenism in the United States. It includes, among others, the following documents useful to us:

1) *An Exposition of the conduct of the two houses of G. G. and S. Howland, and Le Roy, Bayard and Co, in relation to the two frigates Liberator and Hope*. In answer to a Narrative on that subject by Mr. Alexander Contostavlos. By William Bayard (New York 1826, 47 pages).

2) *An examination of the controversies between the Greek Deputies and two mercantile houses of New York*. By John Duer and Robert Sedgwick (New York 1826, 179 pages).

3) *Report of the evidence and reasons of the award between J. Orlandos and A. Louriottis, Greek Deputies, on one part, and Le Roy, Bayard and Co and G. G. and S. Howland on the other part*. By the Arbitrators (New York 1826, 72 pages).

4) *A Vindication of the conduct and character of Henry D. Sedgwick against certain charges made by the hon. Jonas Platt together with some statements and inquiries intended to elicit the reasons of the award in the case of the Greek Frigates*, by the attorney Sedgwick (2nd edition, New York September 1826, 96 pages).

5) *Refutation of the reasons assigned by the arbitrators for their award in the case of the two Greek Frigates*, also by attorney

Sedgwick. (New York, November 1826, 57 pages).

In argument, Alexandros Kontostavlos wrote two works:

1) *A narrative of the material facts in relation to the building of the two Greek frigates*. New York, 1826, 88 pages (2nd edition With a postscriptum by R. Sedgwick, New York, 1826, 96 pages).

2) *Τα περί των εν Αμερική ναυπηγηθεισών Φρεγατών*, Αθήναι 1855.

Finally, also the philellene Palma, whom we have already met, wrote a valuable report on the issue published by *The Times* on 12 September 1826, and then *The Times* devoted to the construction of American ships another investigation on 9 November.

* * *

The government, by decree of 12/24 August 1824, had instructed the Commissioners in London to provide as soon as possible the supply of eight frigates of 18 guns each. The Commissioners considered likely that this provision could be obtained under the best conditions in the United States, and requested information to Bayard, chairman of the philhellenic committee and director of the renowned shipyard Leroy, Bayard and C. Bayard replied that a frigate of 1500 tons and 50 guns of the kind in use in the United States would cost just $ 247,500[69] (or 1,237,500 Francs), and that his company was ready to execute the order quickly.

Consequently, the Greek Commissioners and the London Tetrarchy sent the French General Lallemand to New York in March 1825 to make arrangements with Leroy, Bayard and C. The choice of Lallemand was strange, because having been a cavalry officer, he was no specialist in nautical matters, and he was also awarded a £ 120 monthly compensation, excessive from every point of view. According to the report of Palma, "Without any doubt the choice of a more judicious representative, who could be found for a monthly fee of less than 120 Pounds, would be happier than that of a cavalry officer, former lieutenant of Napoleon, with the mentality of the great enterprises; but the choice was suggested by a group of influential philhellenes." Later, there was a second scandal like this: The manufacturers appointed an inspector of works on their own initiative, a former officer of the American fleet, Chauncey, for $ 12,000 per year (60,000 Francs). The salary of this would be paid by the Greek Government, intentionally not informed about.

---

[69] See the detailed preventive budget by Bayard in *Narrative* by Kontostavlos, page 5.

A. The Independence Loans (1824-1825)

The shipyard started building two frigates of 50 guns as according to the conditions of the offer, to be completed in six months time limit, within which six other smaller ones would also be constructed, to meet the letter of the order of the Greek Government.

In reality, the works began only for the two larger frigates, and the Commissioners in London got to see that the time passed, but neither the communications relating to the delivery of ships nor signs of life from the builders arrived. Having written requesting information, the two received in reply only a new request for money, after they had already sent £ 155,000. Desperate, they turned to Alexandros Kontostavlos, a merchant of Chios, known for honesty and patriotism, who at that time was in London, and begged him to go to America to seek credit with which to complete the two frigates, or at least to sacrifice one of them to save the other[70].

Arriving in New York in April of 1826, Kontostavlos found the situation even worse than expected. The ships were very far from being finished, and the builders demanded $396,060 just to finish one of them. The sum included $261,840 needed for the proper construction, $73,258 in compensation of 20% on an unpaid note of Ricardo and other claims[71].

If not satisfied, the manufacturers were threatening the auctioning of two incomplete frigates, even using the pretext of Article 3 of the American law of 20 April 1818, under which anyone who had ordered the construction of a ship in the U.S. then intended to be used by a sovereign or a state against another sovereign or state with whom the United States were at peace (this was the case of the Ottoman Empire), was sentenced to a fine of not less than $ 10,000 and imprisonment of up to three years. In addition, the ship and its equipment were confiscated by the U.S. government. Indeed, as noted later by the philellene Webster, under the law to which they threatened to resort, the manufacturers would also incur the same penalties; but it was noted that at that time, a frigate and a two-mast vessel ordered by Colombia and Sweden were auctioned at vile prices (70,000 and 32,200 U.S. dollars); it was only to be expected

---

[70] See the instructions given to Kontostavlos in *Τα περί των εν Αμερική ναυπηγηθεισών Φρεγατών*, pages 19-26.

[71] See *Report of the evidence and reasons* pages 8 - 9, *Examination of the controversies*, pages 138 and 149, *Narrative* pages 40, 41 and 61.

that the sale of the two Greek ships was devoted to this unfortunate outcome.

Desperate, having poor knowledge of the language, without acquaintances in a commercial environment that was ill disposed toward him, and already hit by numerous slanders[72], Kontostavlos made the happy choice of going to Washington to try to involve the American government. With the help of Edward Everett, a gentleman member of Congress to whom he had been recommended by Korais[73], Kontostavlos managed to report to U.S. President Adams and explain to the president and ministers what had happened. In the philhellenic and progressive Washington environment, the merchant of Chios was finally able to find an audience motivated by feelings of sympathy: Our homeland was given particularly useful services by the well-known philellene Webster and by Senator Colonel Benton, who said to Kontostavlos: "To the time when I studied Homer, I never imagined that there would come a day when I would make myself useful to his descendants." And generally, the enthusiasm of the people of Washington for the memory of the noble deeds of our ancestors was indescribable. All listened with tears in their eyes to Kontostavlos' stories of the war. And Webster, a famous lawyer, never wanted any reward for the extensive legal advice[74] that he gave.

The government and parliament were shocked to learn the facts of New York, so they did not hesitate to compromise the principles of neutrality to give aid to Greece, and twelve days after the arrival of Kontostavlos in the Capital, the two houses of parliament voted in favour of the acquisition of the second Greek frigate, thereby financing the completion of the first. In the Senate, the proposal spokesman was Colonel Benton.

The U.S. government spent $ 250,000 for the second frigate, which was the right price, though claims of the shipyard to complete the first reached the $396,000: To understand how this figure was formed, we shall consider that the company even had the inconceivable impudence to demand a commission on the business with the U.S. government. Hence, the launch of the Greek frigate

---

[72] See *Examination*, page 157.

[73] The text does not specify better, so this should be understood as Adamantios Korais (1748-1833) (Editor's note).

[74] *Τα περί των εν Αμερική ναυπηγηθεισών Φρεγατών*, pages 36-37.

remained impossible. Kontostavlos, who could behave wisely and cleverly, managed to persuade the American government not to refine the purchase of his frigate before the manufacturer had completed and launched the Greek one, and then asked for an arbitration committee to settle the differences with the manufacturer.

But the arbitrators, rather than blame the manufacturer for the wilful misconduct and the obvious fraud in the preventive budget subjected to the Greeks to get the contract, and for the stratagems by which they managed to miss one after another on all of the commitments taken, simply resized the pretensions from \$396,090 to \$156,856. Henry D. Sedgwick, attorney of Greece, said to the chairman of the arbitration, Jonas Pratt: "Sir, you have done all that was in your power to ruin a country and disgrace another." And the bad faith of the builders seemed obvious even to *The Times*, who in an article on 9 November 1826 observed that the frigate *Brandywine*, built in top-quality oak for the U.S. government and fully armed, cost only \$ 273,000 (1,365,000 Francs), and instead the only ship that eventually would be able to sail from New York to Greece was to cost more than 150,000 Pounds, or 3,750,000 Francs, i.e., nearly triple the Brandywine, which was also better in every aspect. In that article, the referee Pratt was described as the "American Solomon", and was also described the care with which he dealt with the fee of \$ 4,500 for him and the other two members of the arbitration[75].

Fair or not, that was the decision of the arbitrators; in any case, it allowed them to table the complex issue and allowed the Greek people to have at least one new ship. The frigate *Hellas* departed from America and arrived in Nauplia after fifty days' journey, in November 1826. This success was entirely owed to the zeal and judgment of Kontostavlos, who also risked his life in the return journey when mercenary sailors[76] mutinied, and who, having just arrived in Greece, received the official expression of deep and heartfelt gratitude of the Greek people[77] by the Administrative Commission of the island of Aegina, together with an allowance of £ 400 for travel expenses in America, but in a few years saw his merits

---

[75] See *Refutation of the reasons assigned by the arbitrators for their award in the case of the two Greek Frigates del Sedgwick* and the *Report of the evidence…* published by the arbitrators, where they claim to have received a more moderate compensation, page 67.

[76] See *Τα περί των εν Αμερική ναυπηγηθεισών Φρεγατών*, page 113.

[77] Ib. at page 128 the official document.

forgotten, and had his remaining time to live embittered by malignant calumnies and slanders of every kind.

How much damage we have caused with the costume to slander the servants of the nation, can be appreciated by observing that in general, the best men have also avoided having to do with the administration of public economy, for fear of accusations and slanders. For example, in 1878 Peroglou, who lived long in London and was a distinguished person and a lover of the homeland, did not agree to represent Greece in the negotiations for the conversion of the Independence Loans because, he said, he felt unable to deal the task of responding and defending himself against subsequent claims and malignancies, which he considered unavoidable[78].

A.2.3. *Money came into the hands of the Greeks*

Of the total 1,150,000 Pounds available from the second loan, 232,558 escaped the clutches of British and American speculators; it is less than the case of the first loan, when 308,000 Pounds in cash reached Greece in the total of 348,000. The difference between the administration of the first loan by the Philhellenic Committee and that of the second one by the Tetrarchy is quite evident.

The second loan funds transferred to Greece consisted of:

- 182,400 Pounds sent directly to the government;
- 13,108 Pounds carried by the English Gordon;
- 3,350 Pounds carried by Gerostathis for the defence of Missolonghi;
- 33,700 Pounds used for the payment of government bills, which we consider as having been sent to Greece, because they were used as payment for expenses actually approved by the government.

The use of the money that was made in Greece was not different than that of the previous time, which I tried to describe while retaining the pity due to the sins of our heroes. It is needless to repeat the same description for the second loan. But to give an idea of the turn things had taken, suffice it to say that selfishness and propensity to civil war had come to the point that of nearly five million Francs available, not even a penny had been reserved for the defence of

---

[78] See the *White Paper, Λευκή Βίβλος, Μετατροπή των δανείων του 1824 και 1825*, pages 10-11.

Missolonghi, and that when unexpectedly the time came to find resources to help that town, the remnants of the banquet had to be transported from London, 3,350 Pounds, entrusting a simple citizen, the Corfiot Gerostathis, because nobody had confidence in any of the notables.

* * *

We have seen that the total expenditure chapters in which the second loan is divided left off the last 29,022 Pounds, of which 11,600 were used for travel and lodging for three years in Europe of the Commissioners, and the rest was used for certain expenses more or less important, or was lost. There were, among the expenses, a commission payable to a certain Bonfils for 4,800 Pounds, then criticized as improper by the Court of Auditors and by Spaniolakis because fees had already been paid to Ricardo, but that the two Commissioners claimed to be referring to negotiations that happened before the granting of the loan. Out of curiosity, here are some small costs documented in the *Apology*: £ 80 to a Mr. Victor for services rendered to Greece, £ 8 for printing a letter from the Greeks to Philhellenes; to Mr. Revault for a journey to Greece and fees, 170 Pounds, £ 90 to Blaquière for services received; to N. Kefalas were given *on loan, to cease giving trouble to the Commission*, 30 Pounds, and there were other similar expenses. Finally, 2,700 Pounds were lost in the failure of the company Mavrogordatos and 1,700 in transport from London to the port of Falmouth, Cornwall.

A residual availability remained in the hands of Orlandos and Louriotis. The verification of this caused a vehement controversy between the two Commissioners and Spaniolakis, and then gave occasion to a long case before the Court of Auditors, where the issue was complicated to an unimaginable degree. Shedding light on these details is not the task of this book, but I want to mention that I tried to do it only to satisfy a personal curiosity. After fifteen days of study, I was convinced that the utility obtainable from the survey was entirely disproportionate to the effort made necessary by the passed time, by the scarcity of information on the facts and people, and especially by the labyrinthine structure of the two volumes of the *Apology*. In summary, the charges brought against Orlandos and Louriotis concerned: 1) the payment of the fee of 4,800 Pounds to Bonfils, 2) not being able to get 10% discount on supplies of ammunition, 3) the unnecessary and harmful buyback of thousands of bonds, and 4) the failure to treat fairly the affair of iron cannons. For all of this, on 14 January 1835 the two were declared by the Court of Auditors to owe together the sum of 28,769 Pounds and 17 shillings, or Drachmas 809,008.18. The judgment, however, was never executed, and my impression is that the condemnation of the two Commissioners was not right, except perhaps for the commission paid to Bonfils. The other charges were part of the large number of errors that the two committed in London in the context of a situation beyond their control, and that Spaniolakis insisted to charge them motivated by personal animosity.

Therefore, the second loan was lost in the events in London and America: Even ships that managed to get to Greece arrived too late to be useful, and the cash that came in Greece served to feed the seeds of civil war. As evidence of the situation at home, it is useful to mention a story of Missolonghi, to cope with whose siege on 24 December 1825 it was decided to contract a new debt of a million Spanish Piastres. As stated in the decree of the government, "This loan will be guaranteed by security of the nation, i.e. by mortgage on part of the national property of any kind located anywhere in the Greek territory - the mortgage will be in proportion to the mass of domestic goods present in every province, and will not surpass in any the sum of one hundred thousand Piastres - the mortgage of every part of the property will be awarded to the highest bidder at public auction – to the lender will be paid of the annuities of assets under mortgage, except that he shall pay regularly the tithe to the government, like private owners - the loan will last six years, after which the government will return money to lenders by paying eight percent interest per year. Otherwise, it will deliver to providers the mortgaged goods, releasing a regular title to property – the reimbursement will be for half cash, and half in treasure tickets of any kind, or in domestic bonds."[79]

This project, which would deserve a place of honour in the Museum of Finances if it existed, was not successful[80], as it was fate; since on 7 April 1826 the National Assembly of Epidaurus commissioned D. Romas, P. D. Stefanos and K. Dragonas to seek a loan of 100,000 Piastres in the Ionian Islands for the rescue of Missolonghi and for the mobilization of the fleet, to which at least a month's salary had to be paid. Despite the leeway granted to them, the three were unable to find anything, although they had established a commission in 1824

---

[79] Complete Greek and French text in Fabre, *Histoire du siège de Missolonghi*, pages 346 – 351.

[80] Ib., page 229.

that was able to supply useful service in various ways. According to Kampouroglos[81], the committee had been able to send food and ammunition to besieged towns, to find provisional loans and to discount bills of the Government in Zakynthos. It managed to get two loans of 20,000 and 10,000 Piastres and to discount different bills, one of which of 1,500 Pounds[82], and with this money it was possible to rescue starving women and children and to redeem a number of prisoners. This commission also managed to weave relationships with philhellenic officers in the army of Ibrahim, and its members were the first to conceive the idea to ask for British protection and to write the text of the report sent to London. There are no sufficient documents on the work of the Committee during the search of the loan for Missolonghi, whose fall made the consequences of mismanagement of the British loan increasingly clear.

---

[81] See the Introduction of the *Αρχείον Ρώμα*, especially pages 189, 230 and 249.
[82] See ib. page 276.

A.3. Settlement of Independence Loans

The dilapidation of the Independence Loans led also to the unavoidable suspension of their service, i.e. payments of interest and amortization. The affair lasted for sixty-plus years, during which Greece did not refuse to acknowledge its commitments, although this was stated by many, but it tried to adjust its debts through transactions with creditors. That the nominal subscribed capital was repaid, was an hypothesis not considered by even more demanding lenders, given the fragile state forces, the very small advantage that it had taken from loans, and given the fact that the Greek state, having been emancipated after the Independence War, was a separate entity from the government that had contracted debts, and so it could disregard some or even all the obligations of the Provisional Government.

The debts, indeed, had been contracted by assemblies in which were represented many provinces that had taken part in the war, but then had failed to escape from the foreign yoke, and were left outside of the borders of the tiny new country[83]; among them Chios, Samos, Crete, Epirus, Thessaly, Macedonia, etc. The public opinion wondered if it was fair that the new Kingdom of Greece repaid the debts of the provinces remaining under Turkish suzerainty, or whether it was legitimate to treat the providers of the loans of 1824 and 1825 the same way as speculators whose gambling was only partially successful. Several of our citizens[84] supported this argument, and although from a legal point of view they were wrong, it was impossible not to give weight to their assessment. From a legal point of view they were wrong, because in 1824 and 1825 all national land properties were pledged as guarantee to lenders, and all Greeks made themselves jointly and severally liable, so that the national property of the liberated provinces were to be regarded as a guarantee of the entire debt. At the time of the negotiations of 1879, however, Gennadios premised to its plan to convert debt a double card of Greece, in which he showed in colour the disparity between the provinces that took part in the struggle for Independence and

---

[83] See any map of the Kingdom of Greece after 1830 (Editor's note).

[84] See Leventis' booklet, pages 7-9, of little value and full of inaccuracies, but published also in French by the author.

those within the borders of the Kingdom, but the Foreign Minister of the time, Diligiannis, preferred not to use this argument when dealing with foreigners, judging it counterproductive.

Still others wondered if the Greek Government could be considered freed from any obligation for the recognition of liabilities, due to the fact that those contracts had been signed by an insurrectionary government not recognized by foreign powers; it was wondered whether in this case in general a new government set up many years later was jointly and severally liable by the acts of a provisional one. In my opinion, the formula of Politis is valid[85]: "When a Government by law or by force, is settled in power and becomes accepted, or at least tolerated, by the nation, it represents the country and is responsible for the acts of this, irrespective of whether or not the previous Government was recognized diplomatically by other Powers." And consequently, I believe that the acts of the Independence Governments obligated the free Greek state, a consequence that is all the more compelling when we consider that under the moral point of view, the new state should recognize as an obvious thing that it owed its existence to the provisional governments.

Still wanting to argue in the abstract, one could say that it is impossible for a government not recognized, and therefore theoretically nonexistent, to assume obligations which are legally binding on all of its descendants. But, as said Sarrut[86] to everybody who used to conceive government in similar terms,

> A government is not a theoretical abstraction, a simple legal entity.... A government is primarily a power, a driving force, setting in motion the whole machinery of the state, an authority that commands and is obeyed .... No matter whether it is recognized or not by foreign states .... In such matters it is mostly facts that are to be considered.

Anyway, the issue was never in these terms, because Greece — and this goes to its credit — never took advantage of these disputable interpretations to deny its status as a debtor.

Moreover, the debt had been ratified by the National Assemblies not just once. On 8 April 1827, the National Assembly convened in

---

[85] *Les Emprunts d'Etat en Droit International*, page 135.

[86] See his relation about the Balmaceda proceeding and the consequent decision of the French Cour de Cassation against Clunet, 1891, pages 868 – 904.

Troezene began to discuss the signing of a loan of five million Piastres, whose execution would be delegated to the government. The act passed by the Assembly specifically stated that this new loan would be contracted without prejudice to the creditors of the previous loans, and that it would also serve to contribute to the payment of interest. A little later, on 26 July 1829, the fourth National Assembly at Argos decreed that "the Government will take care of the foreign debt as soon as possible, taking into account what was designed in this regard. Behaving in accordance with justice and equity, the government will proceed to negotiate with the holders of 1824 and 1825 debt securities, with the honest purpose of redeeming the nation from debt in general, and national land from mortgages to which they are subject on account of the debt."[87]

The project that is referred to included the formation of a committee composed by Zografos, Papadopoulos and Kontoumas, which would examine the debt situation and would formulate a plan for amortization. On 2 April 1829, the committee submitted its report to the government, in which the serious problem of amortization was examined, and it was estimated that on the one hand to meet debt service would be impossible for six or seven years, but on the other hand, non-payment of interest would diminish the credit of Greece and would make the situation even more difficult. Hence the need for a transaction, and the examination of many possible plans, the most favourable of which provided to the creditors: 1) the buyback of a certain amount of bonds at about 20% of the nominal value, and 2) the announcement of the conversion of one-third of the remaining into a consolidated debt at 5%, and repayment of the remaining two-thirds over a period between 50 and 100 years, drawing lots for the series to be redeemed, according to the system in use in the Netherlands.

Here the commission rightly observed that without a new loan, there would be no resources for the repurchase of an adequate quantity of old bonds, and that if a new loan were granted, the bonds of the old one would immediately rise to a rate well above 20% of original value. As for the second point, in the opinion of the

---

[87] See the Proceedings the Independence Parliament, page 61. The approved text was reproduced in a public document, whose editor modified it by translating it into katharevousa, considering inelegant the language of the Assembly.

commission, the proposal was not to be taken into account, as it was not sufficient to consider the commitments respected, and in any case would not be accepted by creditors.

Therefore, the board proposed an alternative scheme, whose device was rather curious. And that is, that the government would agree with creditors to pay them an interest of 2% on real[88] capital of the old debt, and would borrow £ 444,960 to 5% which had to be lent to 8% to municipalities, provinces and solvent private citizens. Given the difference of the two rates, the government would receive an annual income of 35,596 Pounds, of which 25,052 would be used to pay 2% interest on old debt, and the remainder would be used to redeem the maximum possible amount of it on the stock exchange at current listing. Meticulous and detailed calculations showed that in this way amortization of the old debt would happen in 42 years, while the amortization of the new one gave little thought to the commission, which was sure that the continuous progress of public wealth would easily solve every problem by itself[89].

We need not waste words to refute such a plan, which now should be considered just as an archaeological curiosity. Shortly afterward, however, was proposed a much more serious plan, involving the redemption of Independence Loans by granting to the creditors part of the public estate in Gastouni[90]. It is likely that by that time, the merchants of London overestimated much the value of national lands; Even the French Foreign Minister de Broglie[91] erroneously attributed to them a value of 40 Francs per stremma[92] in average condition. This solution would be almost free of cost for Greece at the time, given the abundance of national lands in relation to the scarce population, and would include in itself the advantage of the immigration of a number of experienced farmers. So it was approved, and not only once, by the National Assembly, e.g., on 20 July 1829, when a resolution passed according to which had to be provided "the allocation of national land in the best way to join the

---

[88] *Pragmatikòs*: obviously is to be understood the effective capital paid, therefore 59% and 55½% of the nominal capital of the old loans (Editor's note).

[89] Details in Mamoukas, vol. 11°, pages 584 – 602.

[90] In the province of Elide, near Patras (Editor's note).

[91] See bibliography.

[92] A tenth of a hectare, i.e. 1.000 m^2 (Editor's note).

national interest with the certainty of foreign and domestic debts."

Unfortunately, the process of negotiating the new Sixty Million Loan was just starting, and the three Protecting Powers had already decided, not without controversy among them, to ensure its service through the most important sources of entry of the Greek Government, taxes and fees on national lands; therefore, the Powers officially stated that before the arrival of regents, the Assembly "neither should decide any sale of national lands, nor should be undertaken any action that could harm the economy of the new state."[93]

Inspired by similar scruples, the regency hesitated to settle the issue by the granting of national lands, the only realistic means. But a few years later, any kind of transaction became impossible, first because the budgets were so lean that an increase of even one million a year in spending would mean an 8% increase of the whole spending, and then because to resume the service of Independence Loans would imply also the resumption of service for the Sixty Million Loan, which had been suspended and whose vicissitudes we are going to describe later in the book.

The situation remained constant in these terms for the whole kingdom of Othon, but the need to reach an agreement with creditors never ceased to be felt[94]. In fact, the Independence Loans, which had been contracted by acts of the Provisional Government that committed us, had been of some use to the achievement of the goal, and were obtained largely through the philhellenic spirit spreading through Europe. The dignity of Greece demanded that they were honoured, as harsh as were the conditions under which they were concluded[95], and their disregard was a stain that would justify all

---

[93] See the Proceedings of the Assembly at Pronoìa, page 23, and Parish, *The Diplomatic History of the Greek Monarchy*, pages 203 sgg. and pages 65-70 of the Annex.

[94] The reasons why Greece should come to an agreement are thoroughly exposed in a pamphlet published by Edward Haslewood, president of the Association of Greek bondholders. See *A letter to his excellency A. Coumoundouros, minister of finance in Greece*, 27 August 1858.

[95] So the Minister of Economy Iannopoulos in a report presented to the king on 6 June 1866. See *Rapport de M. Jannopoulos, ministre des finances, à S. M. le roi George*, traduit et commenté par Ph.

kinds of gossip and slander against our nation. We must consider that it was believed abroad that the prosecution — and finally the happy outcome — of our war were eminently owed to 1824 and 1825 loans. We know that things did not happen like this, but back then, after a few years the scandals in London and New York were forgotten, and that interpretation, repeated incessantly by the creditors of Greece, came to be universally accepted as truth. So About says: "Those loans allowed Greece to conquer its Independence."[96] *The Financier* (18 June 1877) mentions "the bad faith of Greece to the foreign creditors whose money founded its national independence." And Drucker: "These loans have been of much greater benefit to the borrowing country than any other loan contracted in this century; according to the most authentic authors, the Greeks where sinking when the arrival of large sums restored their spirit of resistance and hope for success."[97] An echo of this theory is also inside a well-documented and recent work, *Turkey in Europe* by Odysseus[98]. Years passed, and the attitude also changed in *The Times*, which had once fought so vigorously against the Tetrarchy and American shipyards, and that instead on 3 December 1863 spoke of Greek "bad faith," as well as the *Punch* on 13 Next: *Spell five letters in "Bully, Bilk and Sneak Repudiator, Trickster" read it .... Greek.*

Nor was the question merely ethical. Our first bankruptcy had excluded Greece from the stock markets of the West, and had deprived our young state of the most useful of all goods, credit. As an anecdote, when King George after his coronation came to visit London on 2/14 October 1863, in the capital was held a meeting of creditors of Greece which expressed many benevolent wishes, but in which the President Haleswood was heard even to utter the phrase: "We hope that now Greece will recognize that credit is a source of life for peoples."[99] And in Greece, in fact, without the contribution of foreign capital, neither public works could be made nor communications could be improved, nor banks be founded, and even private companies had no way to progress. Nor could the country think to strengthen the navy or the army.

Goussios, page 28

[96] Page 135.

[97] *An appeal to the governments and monarchs of Europe*, page 3.

[98] Pages 318 – 319.

[99] See the newspaper *Ethnofylax* of 25 October 1863.

Today, seeing the use — or rather, the abuse — of public debt, many idealize the time when the problem did not arise because we had no credit an could not borrow. But at that time, there was no way to develop projects of public utility, or to cope with sudden and unforeseen needs. We saw this well at the time of the great revolt of Crete, when the state was put under terrible pressure by the need to help the refugees who came from Crete in the continent, and by the fear of a Turkish attack. The *laudatores temporis acti* who believe that before defining the old debts the Greek Government was not able to borrow any money, are mistaken. It simply was not able to borrow to the European market conditions, as shown by the long series of domestic lending contracts to heavy conditions signed between 1863 and 1878, only for the lack of access to a wider market.

Considering all of the factors that made it desirable, it seems strange that the final settlement has been delayed so long. But the delay can be explained. Before the change of dynasty in 1863, the transaction was always impossible, but after that year, reaching a solution appeared easy because a definitive agreement on the loan of the three protecting Powers had been reached, because the national wealth had grown, and because the need to open the doors of foreign stock exchanges was felt. But the matter got complicated because of the Greek request to associate the transaction on the Independence Loans with the granting of a new loan, and because of the irrational claims of certain creditors. The bonds were, in fact, in the hands of some Dutch people who had purchased large quantities for speculation, and who now were trying to exploit the need for Greece to recover its good reputation.

It is not known when the Greek bonds had passed into Dutch hands; perhaps this occurred soon after the release of the loan, when money was plentiful and interest very low in the Netherlands. However, there isn't any mention of Dutch bondholders either in English newspapers of the time or in the writings of Orlandos, Louriotis and Spaniolakis. It is certain that the handover took place before 1847, because in his book that came out that year, Leconte says: "Almost all bonds have passed into the hands of Dutch speculators. They are trading to 5 1/4 until 6 3/4% of the nominal capital on the Amsterdam market."[100] According to Gennadios[101], these Dutch were

---

[100] See C. Leconte, *Étude Économique de la Grèce* , page 185.

about thirty people, none of whom possessed a large amount of bonds, with the exception of the speculator Louis Drucker, who had raised nearly half of all circulating bonds, and who visited Greece several times and wrote several memoirs on the issue, in various languages[102]. Until 1874, Drucker maintained some restraint, but since then, he changed his mood. The president of the foreign bondholders, E. Pleydell Bouverie, wrote of him: "There is a Dutch gentleman, named Drucker, who is interested in the issue since years and has published several booklets, by reading which you would believe him an Englishman; namely, an Englishman of a well defined social class, because reading his writings you will find just the usual vocabulary of the fish - market there's near my house."

During the years spent in the accumulation of such controversy, the situation had become worse, and gradually, while the debt increased due to the accumulation of interest and the resources of government dwindled, creditors became more demanding. To understand that the situation had to find a way out was a young chargé d'affaires in London, Ioannis Gennadios. A good diplomat, mastering the English language, and a good writer, he put pressure on the British public as on the Greek Government by means of reports and articles to persuade them both to recognize that they had common interest in a final transaction[103]. It was he who managed to put together an acceptable agreement with the creditors respecting the interests of the state; so, to give due honour to the merit of Gennadios, I'll now describe in detail the path of negotiations for the final transaction.

Theoretical during the whole reign of Othon, negotiations began to take consistency as George's era began, for the reasons we've seen. Immediately after the Congress of the bondholders in London, the new king being not yet installed, in Athens a lively journalistic controversy developed, focused mainly on the question whether the loans had been useful to Greece or not. The newspaper *Elpis* insisted on their infertility, but Merlin, a representative of the bondholders,

---

[101] See *White Paper*, page 69.

[102] See especially *Quelques documents relatifs aux emprunts helléniques contractés à l'étranger*, publiés par L. D. 1e série, La Haye 1874. — 2e série, Leide 1877.

[103] Much of the information on the negotiations that led to the agreement are drawn from a sleek and glossy report by Gennadios of 17/29 December 1875.

opposed to it in the columns of *Ethnofylax*; shortly afterward, a Greek living in London, Pappas, suggested in an article that a loan of two million was contracted to repay Independence Loans and make new resources available. But it took three more years before we began to see some official initiatives. In 1866, for the first time, the Minister of Economy Christidis addressed to Merlin a proposal via the Greek Ambassador Spartalis, suggesting the reduction of capital owed to 16 million, the payment of 36 annual instalments of 960,000 Drachmas, of which 800,000 for interest at 5% and 160,000 for 1% amortization, in exchange for the granting of a new loan of 25 million[104]. The bondholders responded to Minister Kechagias, who by then had replaced Christidis, that they would accept the conversion of the old loan into a new of £ 800,000 to 8%; they would grant a new loan of 1,100,000 Pounds nominal and 880,000 real always to 8%, and that would be necessary to provide an adequate amortization to ensure the extinction of both debts in a definite time.

The counterproposal was not considered adequate, and was officially rejected despite the great urgency brought about by the revolt of Crete in 1867. A private letter from Prime Minister Trikoupis of 21 December 1866 asked the ambassador in London to seek a loan of two million and a half effective to 8%, but the ambassador immediately replied, on 2/14 January 1867, that countries like Egypt, Chile, Peru and Brazil found credit in London only to the effective interest of 10 or 12%, and therefore the conditions in which Trikoupis hoped were impossible to obtain. In the month of August, instructions were given the new ambassador Brailas Armenis to continue negotiations, and as he arrived in London, he wrote a detailed report in which he computed the total debt at 7,466,150 Pounds, including bonds and accumulated interest, against which the British proposed a lump sum of 900,000 Pounds to 8%[105]. Since it was impossible for the government to pay immediately high interest rates, the ambassador suggested starting with 6% in 1868 and increasing by half a year to reach 8% in 1872. The government re-launched, proposing £ 700,000 at 8%, excluding, however, to be able to pay annuities higher than 56,000 Pounds, and expressing its willingness to pledge as guarantee to creditors the incomes of customs, salt pans and other sources of revenue of the

---

[104] For the amortization, see Appendix.

[105] Few above the amount is 800.000: probable misprint (Editor's note).

state treasury. The British, always inclined to avoid issues that are prolonged over long spans of time, agreed with a few minor objections[106], so the deal was finally agreed upon by the parties, and the Greek parliament voted it after the first reading. But the frequent Greek ministerial crises served at once to frustrate everything: the government of Koumoundouros fell almost simultaneously with the signing of the agreement; the next Government Moraitis agreed to continue the settlement, but fell before its ratification, and the still-successive government followed the same fate.

The new Minister of Economy, Valassopoulos, a man of short views[107], did not understand the urgency of the agreement, and having seen the living will to close the question by the British, he thought to show cleverness subordinating again the agreement to the granting of a new loan. The new episode of this style of prevaricating behaviour against creditors, who had already harmed Greece so much, greatly angered the British and deprived us of an unexpected opportunity to consolidate our economy, and ended up justifying the attitude of the Dutch, who, during all the negotiations, had not ceased to mock and insult the British for their magnanimity, and who at this point officially dissociated themselves from the British negotiations and sent to Greece Drucker, who tried to have a hearing directly by the king.

The irritation of the British public did not allow the story to progress for another three years, until on August 1871 Sotiropoulos wrote a confidential letter to the ambassador Brailas, in which he recognized the need to return to the search of a transaction, but stressed it would not be easy to load the Greek budget of other £ 60,000 per year, since the general 44 million debt service weighted already for 5,700,000 Drachmas. So, he proposed to seek a comprehensive solution of all problems by converting the debt into a new one-hundred-million one, thirty of which should be used to guarantee Independence Loans, and the other for internal debt amortization, fluctuating debt and all other obligations of the government. Despite the impediment constituted by the memory of the events of three years before, Economidis was sent to London to

---

[106] See details in the report by Gennadios, page 4.

[107] See circular letters by Valassopoulos of 3 and 24 October 1868, and comments by Gennadios and Spartalis. The policy by Valassopoulos and by the goverments about 1867 was qualified by a ruinous practice of disloyalty.

try to resume negotiations, adding to them another for the founding of a land-credit bank. The overall plan included the conversion to new bonds for 1,000,000 Pounds with 5% interest and amortization of one-half percent, and the payment of 55,000 Pounds per year in the form of shares in the new realty credit; these shares were also guaranteed a yield of 5% by the government. The mission of Economidis[108] lasted under three successive governments without taking a step forward, until finally Gennadios came on the scene.

The situation in which he began to work was certainly worse than what his predecessors had found: Our behaviour in 1868 had cooled every favourable disposition, and the total debt had increased from year to year, reaching the sum of 8,428,975 Pounds in 1875, when Gennadios wrote his long relationship. The progress of the Greek state was evident, and even more so was the growth in the volume of its budget. The need of the influx of foreign capital was increasingly urgent, and the efficiency of the army and fleet were vital stakes in the middle of a crisis in Eastern Europe; thus, in diplomatic circles it was believed that an agreement with Greece would have the favour of English public opinion.

The bondholders demanded the recognition of a consolidated debt of a million and a half Pounds at 5%. Gennadios relaunched, proposing £ 1,200,000 at 5% and a repayment plan, and managed to keep the thread of negotiations without incurring refusals either by the Greek Government or by the British, despite the protests of Drucker. Flanked by other representatives of the government, Malikopoulos (the reason of whose appointment is unknown, since he neither knew English nor had experience in financial affairs), Gennadios came to the following terms of agreement[109]:

1) Independence Loans would be converted into new bonds of the value of 1,200,000 Pounds at 5% interest;

2) These would be distributed as follows: for 100 Pounds of old red bonds of 1825: 31.12 new; for 100 of those blue of 1824: 30.10 new;

---

[108] Regarding this mission, see a long article in *Ημέρα* of 14/26 June 1872, another article in *Κλειοί* of 1/13 July 1872, and pages 6-7 of the report by Gennadios.

[109] The text was published in English: *An agreement with the Hellenic Government for the conversion of the Greek loans of 1824 and 1825*, London 1878, and is translated in English in the *White Paper*, pages 4-7.

for 100 old coupons: 11.12 new. The difference depended on the different expected returns for bonds of the first and second loan, and the ratio was determined by accurate calculations.

3) The amortization would happen in 33 years, with 15,000 Pounds a year. This is a very advantageous condition, since the government had instructed Malikopoulos to require amortization in 40 years, and in 1867 it was forecast to be 50.

4) To limit speculation and disadvantages, the deadline for the conversion of the bonds was one year, after which the old bonds would be forfeited. On this point the government was willing to accept a period of two years, and in 1867 it was expected three.

5) The Greek Government agreed to pay regularly the amounts necessary for debt service. As insurance and guarantees, Article 16 provided that the Greek Government put under mortgage the stamp duty offices, which gave 6 million Drachmas, and the customs of Cephalonia, which gave 1,200,000, to secure the payment of £ 90,000 per year. The government made the commitment not to provide measures that would diminish those sources of public revenue.

This agreement secured the rights of creditors, cleaned up the nation's honour from a bad spot, and opened the doors of the London Stock Exchange to Greek titles: Article 18 expressly provided that the audit committee of the London Stock Exchange would allow the exchange on the Official List of the Greek Government securities, on pain of nullification of the agreement. Given these results, the agreement was welcomed in England[110] as in Greece. Announced on 10 October by the assembly of *Greek bondholders*, the deal was approved by parliament with 82 votes against 18, and the king promulgated it on 8 December 1878. The 18 MPs who voted against it recognized, however, that the agreement was advantageous, and motivated their opposition with the consideration that the Greek budget, in deficit for years, could not bear this additional *phlebotomy*, as wrote the newspaper *Nea Imera* of 14 December.

But in any case, a story was finished, the conversion of the bonds occurred regularly, and from 15 June 1880, the Greek titles were exchanged at London Stock Exchange.

---

[110] See almost all the English press, especially *Daily News* of 11 October, *Bullionist* of 12, *Financier*, and so on. The *Punch* expressly retracted his offensive couplet against the Greeks.

B. The debt under the Bavarian dynasty

The only foreign debts during the reign of Othon were the Sixty Million one and those with Bavaria. During the reign of Othon, the Independence Loans were never recognized, but the service of the Sixty Million Loan and of Bavarians loans weighed on the budget, together with some charges of domestic debt, consisting mainly of compensation and rewards for services received during the war by the Nautical Islands and by other subjects for small amounts. Among the internal debt, there was also a small loan from the National Bank to the Government.

It is necessary to deal separately with all of these issues, because we shall see that they knew several vicissitudes of a different nature, and in particular the debt to the Nautical Islands was only accounted as domestic debt in 1853, and was finally settled just a few months ago, with the law of 16 June 1904.

B.1. The Sixty Million Loan

As expected, the new Kingdom immediately felt the urgent need for foreign credit. Indeed, while the internal productive capacities were exhausted by years of war and were not even sufficient to meet ordinary expenses, the new state was obligated to deal with numerous extraordinary expenditures that were a result of the war, because it could not abandon to their own devices thousands of souls who had sacrificed everything for the nation and who now lacked the daily bread. The situation was this way consistently throughout the time of the Independence War, but became more sensitive after the arrival of Kapodistrias, whose government could survive only thanks to Russian and French money advances and aid. England, taking account of loans granted by its citizens, determined not to be in duty to grant other aid.

According to de Broglie, France had paid around 5,957,000 Francs, of which 500,000 were in loans, in the years between 1828 and 1830[111]. Moreover, France had spent seventeen million Francs for the

---

[111] See de Broglie, page 417. French expenses were exactly:

in 1828, aids in cash Francs 3.588.583 and prisoners ramsons 243.569;

in 1829, aids in cash Francs 1.554.814,20 and prisoners ramsons 1.624.756,86;

maintenance of a fleet in Greek waters near the English and Russian water, but this was an expense that France made only to the benefit of itself and of its prestige. Another 13,335,448 Francs had been spent for the joint benefit of France and Greece for the expedition of General Nicolas Joseph Maison, the *Expédition de Moree*, which later greatly influenced the political events in France.

After the war, the financial needs were evident, but there was no domestic capital available, and there were no foreign lenders willing to take risks after the events of the loans of 1824 and 1825. To find credit, there was no other way than that the three Powers concerned in the founding of independent Greece would sponsor and guarantee a new loan. Fortunately, the Protecting Powers had many reasons for granting this service to Greece. The joint interest of the Protecting Powers and of Greece is perfectly expressed in a letter written by Lord Palmerston to Count Pozzo di Borgo, then Russian Ambassador in London[112], on 14 June 1836:

> From the commencement of the Greek Revolution, one of the greatest difficulties which the Greek nation had to struggle with was the want of pecuniary resources.
>
> A small country in a state of insurrection, and laid waste by a barbarous and desolating war, could have no public revenue; and the accumulations previously made by private individuals were necessarily soon exhausted. Enthusiasm and patriotism enable men to carry on defensive warfare with means far scantier than those of their assailants; but for the achievement of success even in such a contest, pecuniary supplies, to a certain amount, are necessary.
>
> During the civil war, the Greeks were liberally assisted with money by individuals in other countries, who sympathized with them in their struggle for independence; and by such aid the Greek nation was able to maintain the war up to the period when the three Powers agreed, by the Treaty of London, to establish an armistice between the contending parties.
>
> The civil contest then ended; but not with it the pecuniary difficulties of Greece. The expences of military operations ceased, but those of peaceful administration began; and while, on the one hand, the necessary expenditure of peace was much augmented by the number of persons, whose habits had been unsettled by the war. and who, on its termination, were thrown for a time upon the government for support;

---

in 1830, 500.000 Francs advanced, as loan.

[112] See *Papers Relating to the third instalment of the Greek loan*, London 1836, note 18. Text in Parish, Appendix, p. 127.

on the other hand, the sacrifices made by the Greeks in the cause of their country during the continuance of the struggle, and the devastation committed by the Turkish and Egyptian troops upon property of all kinds that came within their reach, had dried up the sources from whence, in other countries, public revenue is found to spring.

It was therefore obvious to all men, that pecuniary assistance from without would be as necessary to Greece during the first few years of peace, as it had been during the continuance of the war. For it was evident, that without a considerable annual income, it would be impossible to organize the several branches of internal administration; to re-establish tranquillity and order; to afford security to persons and property; and to give to agriculture and commerce a rapid and full development; but it was equally evident, that until the several branches or the internal administration were organized; until tranquillity and order were restored; until property and persons were secure; and until agriculture and commerce should revive; no considerable public revenue could be expected to accrue.

For foreigners there continued to exist sentimental reasons to intervene. Philhellenism was still alive in Europe and was not prepared to allow the new state to be left to itself. So, the three Powers were forced to pander to public opinion, by which it was believed that the economic situation of the new state would be strengthened rapidly, and that it would be able to cope with the service of a new loan. According to the Powers the Greek budget expressed in Phoenices, the currency introduced in 1828 and amounted to little less than a Franc, would be the following[113]:

---

[113] See de Broglie, page 403.

B. The debt under the Bavarian dynasty

Incomes	Phoenices
Tithes	3,900,000
Tax on rents	80,000
Customs	2,000,000
Tribunal taxes	100,000
Nautical and passport taxes	59,000
Harbour taxes	70,000
Salt pans	200,000
Pastures	500,000
Tithes on national land	100,000
Land confiscated to Turks	1,050,000
Total (about 7,500,000 Francs)	*8,209,000*

Tab. 5

Expenses	Phoenices
Subsistence of an army of about 11,500 men, whose 3,290 officers	5,360,000
Navy, 44 ships with 1,479 men crew	1,400,000
Ministry of Interior	1,340,000
Ministry of Justice	225,000
Ministry of Public Education	430,000
Ministry of Foreign Affairs and commercial Fleet	27,000
Economic administration, treasury and bank	88,000
Unforeseen expenses	200,000
Total (about 8,200,000 Francs)	*9,070,000*

Tab. 6

The deficit of 861,000 Phoenices, added 3,900,000 Phoenices needed to serve debts, would reach 4,800,000 Francs, to cover which for ten years would be required a loan of 48 million, plus twelve more for the redemption of the north-eastern provinces. According to the French Foreign Minister de Broglie, in this decade the situation was to be stabilized, agriculture and commerce would be increased, and the Greek Government would be able to meet domestic needs and debt service. Furthermore, according to de Broglie, because the national real estate consisted of 10,600,000 *stremmata*[114], six million

---

[114] A tenth of a hectare (Editor's note).

of which arable valuable not less than 40 Francs per stremma, Greece had a wealth asset of 500 million.

There were also political reasons to help Greece, beyond the public opinion Philhellenism. De Broglie said[115]: "I say in summary, that even assuming that France was forced to run some risk in granting the guarantee for the loan, it would be its honour, its generosity, its interest, of course, to take these risks." The foreign Powers were well aware that Greece would not be able to meet its commitments, but while the damage from this was not very much, not exceeding one million per annum for each of them, none of them wanted to run the risk that Greece was attracted to the exclusive sphere of influence of one of the others. This danger was considered important at that time: Each of the three Powers endeavoured by every means to establish political parties favourable to itself in the new kingdom, and to exercise influence excluding the others.

This zeal, now forgotten, is explained if we consider the international situation of Greece at the time, when there were other unredeemed countries in the Middle East and a united and strengthened Italy had not yet appeared on the horizon. Distinguished for the glory of its Independence War, Greece appeared to be the likely successor of Turkey and was considered as the only naval power in the eastern Mediterranean. "Greece," said de Broglie, "soon will hand the keys of the Hellespont." The judgment that we can give today about this perspective is different, because the attribution of such importance to Greece did not correspond to reality and would lead to fatal disillusionment, as soon acknowledged Thouvenel[116], and then because since 1850, i.e., from the time when Philhellenism lost its appeal, the spiritual and material progress of free Greece as of unredeemed could be seen just in their seed: We can get an idea about Greece of the time without consulting newspapers and documents, but simply through the novel *Thanos Vlekas* of Pavlos Kalligas, of 1855.

This is, in brief, the set of reasons that led the Kingdom of Greece to contract new loans. Let's now see how the negotiations were held to contract, how they were used, and what their status is at present.

---

[115] Ib., page 416.

[116] See *La Grèce du Roi Othon*, pages 8-9.

B. The debt under the Bavarian dynasty

B.1.0. Sources of research

With regard to the preliminary negotiations and the granting of the loan, there are several British diplomatic documents, which will be mentioned below, and the following text are particularly relevant:

1) *Sur le projet de loi relatif à la garantie de l'emprunt grec* (8 May 1833) by the Duke de Broglie, at the time French Foreign Minister (the document is in the 2nd volume of his *Discours et Écrits*);

2) A curious script by H. H. Parish, *A Diplomatic history of the monarchy of Greece* (London 1838). The author of this paper was in service for years as a clerk in the British Embassy in Greece, and carefully picked up a wealth of information which, without him, would be long forgotten, or at least would become very difficult to find. But, animated by ardent hatred toward Palmerston, whom he considered intentioned to leave Greece to the Russian sphere of influence, he showed a serious lack of two essential qualities for a historian, acumen and the ability to distinguish.

Concerning the use of the loan, we rely mainly:

1) on the *Balances of the General Economic Management of the state from January 1833 to December 1843* (Γενικοί Λογαριασμοί της οικονομικής διαχειρίσεως του κράτους από Ιανουαρίου 1833 μέχρι Δεκεμβρίου 1843), written by Metaxas, a document particularly credible because it was verified by Lemaire, at the time representing the French Government at our National Bank;

2) on the *Étude Économique de la Grèce* by Leconte, a book published in 1847 after the author had spent two years in Greece, which for the richness and accuracy of the information is one of the most valuable aids to the study of that time;

3) on studies of Mendelssohn - Bartholdy, of Edmond About and Finlay.
Speaking of events of Bavarian administration and army, I mentioned writings and sayings of the Greeks only very rarely, because my readers might consider them unreliable as dictated by the passions of those times, now forgotten.

Finally, with regard to the negotiations subsequent to 3 September 1843 and the subsequent settlement of the loan, information is available mainly in English diplomatic documents and in a French one. They are mostly a few pages of brochures and only partially relevant; however, they are interesting, as they deal with contemporary events. The English documents are mostly publications related to ongoing debates in the House of Commons, while the *Livre Jaune* of 1866 has no internal unity, but contains correspondence exchanged between France and other countries, including Greece. But given the lack of official Greek documents of that time, and given the animosity and pettiness of our parliamentary debates of that time, those British documents are the only slender means by which one can gain knowledge of the question. As for our parliamentary life, by the Senate there was just one frank discussion, that was free of the character of extreme partisanship and pettiness that lasted until early 1860. This is the debate[117] on the report of Senator Chatziskos of 8 March 1860, for the Sixty Million Loan, and it is characterized by moderation and knowledge of the facts.

B.1.1. Negotiations and granting of the loan

In February 1830, Prince Leopold of Saxe-Coburg had expressed the wish that "the High Powers should deign to assure to the new Greek state, until its own resources shall recover their vigour, pecuniary succour proportioned to its wants; the fact being notorious that the Provisional Government has been enabled hitherto to exist only by the subsidies granted by the generosity of the High Powers."[118] Even before then, Kapodistrias had proposed a loan of sixty million to the National Assembly. The fourth National Assembly, at Argos, approved a loan that would serve for the founding of the National Bank, for the settlement of Independence Loans and of foreign requests, and to revitalize agriculture, commerce, shipping, etc.[119]

The request was granted by the London Conference of 1829-30, which established the boundaries of the new state, and in Article 17 of the Protocol of 8/20 February 1830, the delegates declared that "the three Powers decided to provide financial support to new state guaranteeing a loan contracted by the Greek Government, the purpose of which will be to cover the expenses of maintaining the army which the Head of the state will have at his service." Prince Leopold asked that the protocol conditions would be altered so that the loan would serve all of the needs of the Greek state, and not just military ones, and the request was received with a new protocol of 7 May, in which it was stated that the loan would amount to Sixty

---

[117] See Proceedings of the Senate of 22 and 23 March.

[118] See Parish, Appendix, p. 126.

[119] See Μάμουκαν, ια', 151 - 155 και έκθεσιν Χατζίσκου εις την Γερουσίαν τη 8η Μαρτίου 1860, *Πρακτ. Γερουσίας*, σελ. 488.

Million, of which each of the Powers would be a guarantor for one third, and as for its use the Greek Government would be completely autonomous.

Unfortunately, on 21 May 1830, Prince Leopold declined the offer of the Kingdom of Greece, and the matter of the loan did not progress until 13 February 1832, when the choice fell on Othon of Bavaria. Just having solved the problem of the dynasty, the representatives of the three Powers communicated confidentially to the Ambassador of Bavaria the conditions under which Othon should go in exchange for the crown of Greece, among which some concerned the loan: Othon would ensure acceptance of the conditions proposed by Leopold, and the loan would be paid in instalments according to the needs of Greece, which was supposed to pay the interest and amortization using its tax revenues.

The treaty concluded on 7 May 1832 between the three Powers and Bavaria included these conditions, and added[120] that the Head of State and the Greek state would pledge to devote the resources of the public treasury to interest and amortization payments prior to any other expenditure, stating that "the diplomatic representatives of the three Courts would specifically be involved in monitoring compliance with this condition." This is a detail that deserves special attention, as it contains the seeds of the institute of International Control. It is true that this condition of the Treaty of 1832 was never applied; however, the text provided that conditions stipulated by a third party could subject a free state to control by others: The Treaty, in fact, granted the Sixty Million Loan as a result of a negotiation between the Powers and Bavaria, not between them and Greece, and subsequently the loan was considered to be concluded without the Greek people, who were never consulted. This was something completely new, but very characteristic of the later history of our finances.

The loan so guaranteed by the three Powers was delivered by the Rothschild bank in Paris, to the interest of 5% and 1% amortization. The bankers who underwrote the bonds bought them at a price of 94%, recognizing that the investment bank fee of 2% and other compensations. The contract was signed 1st March 1833 in Paris by the Greek ambassador Soutzos[121]. The disbursement of the loan was

---

[120] See article 12, paragraph 6 of the treaty.

[121] The text is reproduced in Parish, Annexes, pages 209-216.

scheduled in three 20 million series, the first two of which were paid very soon, while the third was paid later on account of resistance of Russia[122], at odds with the pro-British inclinations of von Armansperg; Russia at first proposed to pay only part of the third set, then that the payment was conditioned to the regulation of all accrued interest and amortization, and finally it was paid as the previous two, thanks to the intervention of Palmerston[123], on the condition that economies in some chapters of the Greek budget were provided.

B.1.2. Using the loan

Just as had been desired by Prince Leopold, who had wanted that the loan would not be used for military expenses alone but for all kinds of needs of the Greek state, it was hoped by everybody that the loan would give new life the productive capacity of the country, that roads would be constructed, impetus to agriculture would be given, banks would be founded, a solid foundation for public safety would be established, and a small but efficient army would be maintained. The facts, we shall see, entirely dashed these rosy hopes.

The secured loan amounted to 60 million nominal Francs, equivalent to 67,008,000 Drachmas at a rate of 111.68. These bonds were actually issued:

On guarantee	Francs	Drachmas
English	19,838,805	22,155,968
Russian	19,999,573	22,335,533
French	17,400,661	19,433,058
Total	*57,229,040*	*63,924,559*

Tab. 7

French bonds are lower than the other for 2,600,000 Francs that

---

[122] See *Papers Relating to the third instalment of the Greek Loan 1835-6. Presented to the house of Commons. July 1836*, and *Additional Papers relating to the third instalment of the Greek loan 1835-6. Presented to both houses of Parliament. August, 1836*. The negotiations for the third series of the loan show how Russia was then trying to buy the favor of Greece with the millions. There is a document in three letters of Rudhart to Soutsos, then ambassador at St. Petersburg, preserved by the Library of Greek Parliament.

[123] See the communication to count Pozzo di Borgo of 3 June 1836 in *Papers relating…*, n. 17.

France reserved for the payment of interest and amortization of the years 1838 to 1840[124], and to this aim, it took out of circulation bonds for that amount.

Since the loan was awarded to 94%, to the nominal capital of about 63 million Drachmas were to be subtracted:

6% loss on nominal capital	3,835,473
Discount for cash payment	1,186,288
Rothschild 2% commission and other expenses	1,964,252
Total drachmas	*6,986,013*

Tab. 8

Numerous complaints against the Powers were voiced, even in the Greek Parliament, for not having allowed Greece the benefit of more favourable conditions. As for the loan price, the criticism is baseless: Europe was in a time of instability, and money was expensive. We shall not forget that in 1831, France had issued 5% bonds to 84% of their nominal price, and again in 1832[125] to 98.50%. So, Greece benefited from conditions similar to those of France. The Russian economic situation was incomparably worse than the French, and even England was no better, because of the turmoil that followed the reforms of 1832. The Powers could work to ensure better treatment to Greece only as regards the commission of the Rothschild and expenses.

From capital remaining after expenses, 56,948,546 Drachmas, only interest and amortization at 31 December 1843 amounted to 33,080,795 Drachmas: There remained, therefore, only 23,867,751 Drachmas actually exited from hands of the note holders, but alas, even these were not dedicated to the needs of the country. The loan actually disbursed was diminished from 12,531,174 Drachmas due to Turkey for the redemption of the province of Fthiotida (a sum which is suspected even to have gone back into Russian hands[126]), and 2,238,559 owed to several creditors[127] for expenses that occurred

---

[124] See Ἔκθεσιν τῆς Γερουσίας, Senate acts page 492, ἀγόρευσιν Χρηστίδου, ib., page 540).

[125] See Leroy-Beaulieu vol. 2°, pages 598-599.

[126] According to the *Additional Papers*, N° 1 enclosure 1, one-half of this amount, exactly 5.984.235 Drachmas, in reality was paid to Russia. According to Leconte and About (page 277), this sum for damages of war of 1829 ended up entirely in Russian hands.

[127] Precisely: to Russia 1.857.358,03, to Francia 372.666,66, to

before the establishment of the Kingdom. The remaining 9,098,017 Drachmas and 45 cents went to expenses for the Regency and the Army, spending hardly classifiable as useful to the country.

Here it is necessary to insert an observation as clarification. The claim that the capital at 31 December 1843 was reduced by about 33 million in interest, and more by repairs due to Turkey and other amounts, leaving just 9,000,000 available, is taken from the book of Casimir Leconte[128], and is correct because the figure corresponds to an interest payment of about 3.6 million for nine years, as required by contract terms. However, at first it is not easy to understand why one should account the actual remaining available for Greece in 1843 rather than at any other time: The reason why the accounts are exposed in this way is that after 1843 in Greece, the sums were drawn in the already-quoted official report Balances of the General Economic Management of the state from January 1833 to December 1843 *prepared by Metaxas, which indicated a figure of 9,000,000 as theoretically available for economically productive investments, but which was lost, as will be seen immediately below.*

So, the figure is correct, but the exposure is not particularly relevant to focus on the actual problem, which was this: In the face of a state budget of about 10 million in income and expenses (that was envisaged at the end of the Independence War, as we have seen in this chapter), to Greece had been paid the full amount of the Sixty Million Loan (first the 40 million guaranteed by England and France, and shortly after also the amount guaranteed by Russia), forcing the country to spend 3.6 million by way of annual interest and amortization. But this economy had a domestic product (if it could be estimated) at most ten or twenty times bigger than the state budget of ten million: To attempt a very rough estimate, we can consider that Greece had only one million inhabitants and had a state budget of about ten Drachmas or Francs per capita. But as we shall see below, with a few hundred Francs per year a soldier could be fed and armed, and a few dozen Francs was the amount of pensions paid with great difficulty to families ruined by the war, and princely pensions were considered the very few ones which came to hundreds of Francs per month; from this data we can make a statement that the GDP per capita could be on the order of a magnitude of hundred or two hundred Francs, at most.

Then, Greece of the 30s of the nineteenth century might need a few million of funding to be able to invest it in public works, to increase its wealth and to serve the payment of interest and amortization on capital having achieved greater utility than the amount of these, or at least equal to them. Every million borrowed would generate an instalment of 60,000 Francs per

---

banker Eunardos 276.771,91, amortization of an old London loan 381.201,12.

[128] *Étude Économique de la Grèce*, 1847, page 175.

annum interest and amortization, and then to make sense the operation, every million had to be invested in the most urgent public works, capable of increasing the wealth and tax revenue at least enough to pay instalments, if not immediately in a few years. Sixty million in cash did no good to Greece, because its rudimentary administrative apparatus would not be able to invest it in productive public works, or to spend "for the growth of agriculture and commerce" (as it used to be said then) even on the most optimistic assumptions. So, the hypertrophic loan paid altogether could serve to nothing else than partially repaying itself, leaving a heavy burden on the debtor after the consumption of advanced capital. Namely, Greece was in a position to have received net about 50 million Francs and having to pay 36 instalments of 3.6 million to repay them. Once the first 14 instalments were paid, 50 million would be spent, and Greece would have to pay the other 22 with I do not know with what resources, and without any benefit for itself. So, it does not make any difference to calculate the total interest and amortization on any interim date: The actual amount available to Greece was not the remainder of the loan, at any date, 1843 or otherwise, but probably zero, because of the enormity of the sum and consequently of the interest, although this loan guaranteed by the Governments of the three Powers had not been granted to a very high rate, unlike Independence Loans, delivered to 11% effective.

We have also seen (chapter B.1.1) that international protocols with which the disbursement of the loan was decided provided that it be paid in instalments according to the needs of Greece, "to give a kind of starting capital to this extemporary kingdom," according to About's expression[129], but instead the loan was disbursed in one piece, killing the patient like a medicine overdose, and the interaction between several competing factors appears very clear here: the inability of the young independent state to administer the community and defend itself in the negotiations, the credulity of the romantic Philhellenism of foreign public opinion, which had an Arcadian vision of the imagined imminent and great civil and economic development of Greece, the propensity of the Powers to finance the country to build an outpost in the Mediterranean for themselves, and finally, the ease of placement of the loan that Rothschild found in the market, since the loan was guaranteed by the Powers.

For the regency 1,397,654 Drachmas were spent in fees and expenses of travel, stay, accommodation and finally for the return of the regents to Germany. There is little to say beyond a few touch of colour on the customs of the Regency, whose propensity to dissipation was already criticized by one of the three regents, von Maurer, as we read in the only historian who has dealt extensively

---

[129] About, *La grece contemporaine*, page 275.

about that time, Mendelssohn - Bartholdy, who tells us how the regency was trying to impose by force the institutions of the European states to the small Greek world: "To what aim magnificent ministries instead of simple offices that would be necessary; to what aim an entire army of Ministerial advisers and state Councillors who were not even able to advice themselves, and that ended up leaving everything to the provincial offices; to what aim the expenses for uniforms and gaudy titles, to what aim this masquerade, so called by the people, who saw the show as a farce of their own poverty?"[130] Coming to the deeds of von Armansperg in person, the German historian adds: "It cannot be denied that Count Armansperg, even if one is willing to accept as an excuse his immense ignorance in economic matters, ruthlessly took advantage of the Greek state coffer to meet his needs and desires. The expenses only for the abode of regents amounted to 91,000 Drachmas per year (...). To adorn beautifully his palace in Nauplia, Armansperg had not renounced either the harpsichord and the Viennese carriage, or the baldaquin come from Monaco via Marseille, and even the flour needed to glue the upholstery of the walls cost thousand Drachmas to the Greek state. With these measures, the President of the Regency had in mind to provide the Greek people an opportunity to know European grandeur and compare Greek poverty."[131] In Mendelssohn's book, there are also witty satires of the various characters of the Armansperg's court, such as archigeometre Gebhardt, who "would elsewhere be sent to a psychiatric hospital, in Bavaria was used as a substitute, and in Greece was highly regarded by his superior officer and received the annual salary of 4,320 Drachmas."[132]

After 1832 and until 1843, Greece had two armies, one actually Bavarian which King Ludwig had made a commitment to send, and one organized later, known as the Greek army. According to the protocols, Ludwig had made a commitment to send into Greece a body of 3,500 volunteers, but since the enrolment of these did not happen on time, on 1st November 1832, the regents signed with Bavaria a covenant under which Ludwig put at the disposal of his son Othon 3,500 men of regular troops, who went to Greece together with the young king. This expeditionary force proved the lowest

---

[130] See page 138.

[131] See pages 661-662.

[132] Ib., page 663.

utility[133] and cost around 4,748,000 Drachmas for the trip to Greece for the maintenance and the return to Bavaria. The report of the Metaxas tells us that in the period of 1 October 1832 – 30 September 1833, 2,746,067 Drachmas were spent on the journey of the soldiers, and 1,784,283 and 217,700 for their support for the return of those who had already been dismissed. A Frenchman had to consider that "the Greeks had to pay for the Bavarians, and then to pay to get rid of them," and according to Senator Milios (Senate session of 23 March 1860), ammunition and equipment costing 910,067 Francs consisted of any unusable equipment that lay accumulated in warehouses and arsenals of Munich.

After the arrival of Bavarian soldiers, there was hope for rapid progress in the general situation, and it was decided to enrol a Greek army that should be trained by the Bavarians. But the Bavarians, instead of organizing the army, provided directly to compose it with their own men, so that in a country where it certainly did not lack the martial experience of veterans of the Independence War, as was Greece in the summer of 1835, we had an army of 8,205 men, in which almost all of the 5,142 effective were Bavarians. Kyriakidis[134] said that teachers abounded and students were sent home. And Leconte: "It is common knowledge, that the troops recruited in Bavaria were composed of the dregs of Germany and that their conduct in Greece was often strongly reprehensible, and their presence did irritate the populations, made them hostile to the government and created very serious embarrassment."[135] Also Mendelssohn - Bartholdy quotes from the archives of Berlin a note of the Prussian embassy of 18 October 1835: "These troops recruited among the vagabonds from all over Germany are very bad and cost a lot."[136]

The second army, Greek in name and Bavarian in fact, was much larger and more expensive than necessary. The Bavarian volunteers were paid 25 cents a day, but the Bavarian officials were quickly raised to the highest honours. At least according to Finlay, Bavarian officials were so incapable that the government did not dare publish

---

[133] See Mendelssohn – Bartholdy, page 638.

[134] *Ιστορία του συγχρόνου Ελληνισμού*, Vol. 1°, page 293.

[135] Page 185.

[136] Page 637. See also Γ. Αγγελόπουλον, *Λόγοι Πανεπιστημιακοί*, page 52.

their roles (army lists) to cover his bias toward compatriots. Of thirty upper officers, twenty-three were Bavarian and seven Greek or philhellenes, while among 258 lower officers, the Bavarians were 139[137]. Rudhart, Armansperg's successor, in 1837 renewed the contracts with the Bavarian troops — "an unfortunate idea," according to Leconte[138], which "would be sufficient to undermine a reputation more established than his."

Again according to Leconte, in the years 1845 and 1846, 4,400,000 Drachmas were sufficient to maintain the army. Instead, in the eleven years from 1833 to 1843 we find an average expenditure of over 6 million annually for the same army — average spending that reached 7,300,000 Drachmas per year before 1838, the year in which were put into effect significant spending cuts at the request of Powers, which subordinated the payment of the third series of loan to the verification of severe economies in the budget[139]. So, we spent around 67,344,044 Drachmas against the 48 million that would be sufficient to administer the army from the beginning with the criteria adopted in 1845, and so about 19 million were lost in this way. Therefore, the Greek state in 1843, having spent in mediation 6,986,013 Drachmas, 14,769,733 in damages of war, 33,080,795 in interest and amortization and 19 million in the mismanagement of the army, had thoroughly exhausted the loan, not having gotten any benefit for itself, except for the redemption of the north-eastern provinces, obtained at the price of an outlay which, in part, was finished in the Russian coffers[140].

At the cost of sacrifices, and thanks to some extra help for which credit must be given to foreigners, at the date of 1843 all of the debt service had been paid. But from Bavaria were borrowed 4,658,186 Drachmas, of which 2.809.077 returned on 31 December 1843, and the three Joint Powers had given an extraordinary contribution of 2,757,028 Drachmas, which immediately afterward France wanted to double at its charge. With all of this, at that point Greece did not have anything left of the loan, but was in debt of 66,842,126 Drachmas and 46 cents, so much poorer than the day it was forced to

---

[137] Finlay, vol. 2°, pages 116-117.

[138] Page 25.

[139] See the Reports to the French Parliament by Dubois, 21 March, and by Duke de Broglie, 16 April 1838.

[140] See About, page 278.

borrow.

Despite numerous turbulent attempts to modify the financial management, already the year 1842 was closed with a deficit of three million, and then the suspension of interest payments was inevitable. After Regny died, the direction of economy remained in the hands of Tisamenos, who tried to refit the budget by auctioning the national real estate and vineyards in a bad state; but not succeeding, he resigned. Christidis refused to replace him, and then Selìbergos and Rallis succeeded him, and they tried in vain to find credit in Austria but soon recognized that the economic situation had reached the worst of the worst. Ascertaining all of this, the three Powers sent their representatives to a conference in London on 1 May 1843, and determined that there should be annual savings of 3,742,000 Drachmas, and to ensure the interests, stipulated that the right to collect the incomes of the customs of Syros should be given to the Powers. The king had to submit to this protocol, but then it was not applied as a result of political upheavals of the following year, after which the whole payment of interest and amortization ceased.

And thus ended the story of the Sixty Million Loan, and began the long negotiations to settle it.

B.1.3. Negotiations for the settlement of the loan

The negotiations are to be divided into two periods, the one from 3 September 1843[141] until the Occupation of Piraeus during the Crimean War[142], the other following the Crimean War. In the first period, the Powers limited themselves to diplomatic representation. The same governments felt a sense of responsibility in the matter of a loan "contracted without the Greek people were consulted and spent the same way," as Finlay says[143]. So, according to About: "Nobody knows what to admire most, the boldness of Regents, the bonhomie of the Greek people, or the temerity of Powers entrusting sixty million to three particular here had the right to waste them,"[144] and Leconte adds: "Attributing to the Greek government, and more so to the nation, which until 1843 remained completely foreign to the

---

[141] Day of the military uprising for the Constitution (Editor's note).

[142] The Anglo-French occupation of Piraeus lasted from May 1854 to February 1857 (Editor's note).

[143] Finlay, page 238.

[144] About, page 275.

discussion of its own interests, the squandering of helps granted by the protecting powers, would be an injustice so glaring that we do not admit that such feelings could find any place in an enlightened spirit," and moreover, "The Greek position is identical to that of a minor forced, on attaining majority, to fulfill obligations taken on his behalf by a family council; it is from such point of view that these obligations must be considered and that we must ask their extinction."[145]

But the Greek Government, instead of taking all of the necessary steps to reach a reasonable agreement, made mere promises — hoping to take advantage of differences between the Powers — and began to write in its budget amounts that were never paid, with the exception of only one case that was a result of a particular insistence by the English: A situation not much different than that which repeated itself between 1893 and 1897. Instead, after the Crimean War, the Powers could treat Greece at their discretion, and acted observing only the limitations that seemed right to their judgement — a behaviour that reminds us of recent times.

B.1.3.1. Period 1843 – 1856

The period prior to the Crimean war was the one in which the Protecting Powers limited themselves to representations through diplomatic channels. The only somewhat energetic meddling in the issue occurred at the time of Kolettis' Government, when England continually gave trouble to the pro-French party. Among the British, Palmerston was especially acidic, and as opposition leader, he declared that the British Government was entitled to claim the application of the Treaty of 1832, even without the agreement of the other Powers, and to make use of the right to intervene provided for in Article 12, § 6. Prime Minister Robert Peel responded to him in the Parliament[146], not denying the English right to intervene, but

---

[145] Leconte, pages 189 and 340.

[146] The discussion at the House of Commons on 1 August (Parlementary Debates 1845, vol. VI.) made a deep impression in Greece, causing in September del 1845 a parliament debate on the issue, whose Proceedings were soon translated in French and published in order to make them available to the English Parliament. The publication has the title *Une discussion à la Chambre Grecque*. The style of the French publication—mediocre in itself—is, nonetheless, clearly above the level of its content.

expressing the reasons of prudence: "We could not resort to that extreme power which we possess under the treaty, without bringing on a crisis fatal perhaps, to the existence of that popular form of government in Greece, which we have been instrumental in creating and which we are anxious it should continue."[147] Peel rebuked Palmerston to have spoken too harshly about a foreign country and to have made the situation difficult for Kolettis to the benefit of the court of Ali Pasha, at the risk of contributing to the eternal duration of the policy of the tyrant.

But then Foreign Minister Aberdeen exerted great pressure on Kolettis[148] to compel Greece to resume debt service. An acrimonious communication by Aberdeen threatened to use the options provided by Article 12 § 6 of the Treaty of 1832, attributed to Greece to have hypertrophic military spending, and not to be able to suppress banditry and to create difficulties by endeavouring to procure riots in Turkey. Only on one point Aberdeen was willing to compromise: the suspension of amortization payments. Kolettis took time with a very long communication of 20 October 1845, a masterpiece of Eastern diplomacy, the kind of those political masterpieces in oriental style that have always brought evil to Greece, and never good. Aberdeen flew into a rage, feeling teased[149], and Kolettis was forced to succumb before the British protests, on 16/28 February 1846.

Repeated in 1847, the British pressure forced the government to resort to the Greek banker and philellene Eynard for the anticipation of 500,000 Francs, which temporarily silenced Britain, to which were paid throughout 793,552.21 Francs. Eynard was repaid in three instalments between 1848 and 1850, without interest, under a law of 9 December 1847 authorizing the government to deal directly with him so as to agree to the terms of repayment.

Subsequently, on 18/30 August 1847, Kolettis tried to convince the Powers in a public speech that the failure to pay interest had to be blamed on Members of Parliament and Senators, who all sought to reduce taxes, and at the same time made every effort to increase

---

[147] Parliamentary Debates 1845, vol. VI, column 1336.

[148] See *Correspondance respecting the failure of the Greek Government to provide for the payment of the interest and sinking fund of the Greek Loan*, London 1846 (it is an official publication containing some documents).

[149] See letter to Sir Edward Lyons del 10 December.

public spending in their electoral districts. Kolettis declared his intention to find resources through the sale of national estate and buildings, and made a commitment to pay one-third of the interest due in 1848, and gradually to increase the amount paid each year until 1860, when Greece would be able to pay the full interest. As a consequence of these statements, Kolettis enrolled in the budget of 1848 1.278.491 Drachmas, which was exactly one-third of the debt service, and the Minister of Economy Korfiotakis[150] gave very detailed instructions in this regard. According to Finlay[151], these utterances received little attention because "the Protecting Powers had no faith in the sincerity or honesty of the statements of Kolettis," and in 1848 it was not actually paid a penny, and the following year the capital owed ceased also to be mentioned in the budget; previously it had been inscribed in the balance sheet to show that Greece had no intention of reneging on its obligations. In 1852, Greece returned to promise the payment of 400,000 Francs per year to demonstrate its good will — a demonstration that remained platonic, since the amount was enrolled in the budget, but was never paid[152].

B.1.3.2. Period 1856 – 1864

After the Crimean War and the Paris Peace, the Powers, exhausted by the eternal negotiations, fumbled for a way to close the matter once and for all. A committee of three Powers settled in Athens and tried to determine the actual economic conditions of Greece and the amount that could be paid actually by the Greek state. The settlement of the Committee, composed by Thomas Wyse, A. Ozeroff and Charles de Monthérot, was an occasion for justified sorrow for the public, and certain of our politicians, who had very recently held ministerial positions and had not found it indecent to budget amounts they had already decided not to pay, liked to classify the Committee as "incompatible with the dignity of the Greek state." However, the commission submitted its report to the Governments of the Powers on 12/24 May 1859, and, giving very severe judgments on the financial system in general — and in particular on the Greek bookkeeping (which "did not offer any legal guarantee of exactness

---

[150] See Report on Budget of 1848, pages 8-9.
[151] See Finlay, page 205.
[152] See Christidis, discourse at the Senato on 22 March 1860, and About, page 277.

and authenticity") — in regard to the debt of 1832 expressed itself as follows[153]:

> Considered that Greek state revenues are increasing without that the provisions of the Treaties are satisfied;

> Considered that with the increase in revenue expenditures also dilate, without that in the general situation of the country be found any benefit from the annual expenses incurred by the Protecting Powers, neither in the form of encouragement to industry, nor in any other form of initiative that could be taken by the state;

> The Commission, seen also Article XII § 6 of the Treaty of 7 May 1832, has formed the view that Greece is obliged to contribute to the annual costs that are incurred on its behalf.

> As regards the sum of which payout can be requested, the Commission believes that Greece, if well managed, would be able to observe all its commitments, and therefore that the Powers could force it to pay all interest and amortization due without thereby violating any principle of justice.

> Not wanting to create difficulties to the country nor to affect its public services and its development, the Commission proposes to set a lower limit on the contribution due by Greece to 900,000 Francs.

> Forecasting that Government revenues will increase, the Commission believes that this limit can be increased gradually.

It is worth recalling that already on 17 February 1850, in a letter to Gregorios Soutsos[154], Eynard had expressed the opinion that the amount of 900,000 Francs was the maximum that the Powers would be entitled to request in payment. The same conclusion was reached by the Commission, which took into account the legal obligations of Greece, but also the reality of its budget, which by then had reached 15,735,000 Francs.

The conclusions were accepted without discussion by the Powers, which soon began to put pressure on Greece for ratification[155]. After

---

[153] The report was published in French and English by the English Government, under the title: *General report of the Commission appointed at Athens to examine into the financial position of Greece*, London 1860.

[154] Preserved with some other in the private archives of D. I. Soutsos.

[155] See *Papers relating to the Arrangement concluded in Athens in June 1860* (Presented to the house of Commons, in pursuance of their address dated April 29, 1864). London, 1864. On 22 August, Lord Russell wrote to the ambassador in Athens Wyse that the

some negotiations, the Government of King Othon went under the yoke, and on 9/21 June, the Minister for Foreign Affairs Kondouriotis announced that although the proposals of the Powers had diverged significantly from the 300,000 Francs a year that had been budgeted by Greece, the government had accepted them and had also obtained the approval of the Parliament.

Who is aware of the fact that even today, in 1904, we pay 900,000 Francs a year for the Sixty Million Loan, could also believe that the announcement of Kondouriotis had closed the matter once and for ever? It is not so. First, the Bavarian monarchy paid the 900,000 Francs only once, and the change of dynasty found the issue in an outstanding state. Soon afterward, with a notice of 12/24 January 1864, Greece asked Powers to three concessions[156]:

1) deferral of interest never paid in 1861, 1862 and 1863;

2) extension for five years of the agreements of 1859, to ensure Greece that the annual fee would not exceed 900,000 Francs;

3) allowance to Greece to allocate part of its income to repay the Independence Loans, rather than use it in full for the 1832 loan. With the change of dynasty, in fact, as we have seen, negotiations had also begun for the settlement of the Independence Loans.

The Powers[157] agreed to the first two points, asking in return that a branch of the Greek revenue would be devoted exclusively to the annual debt service that was agreed upon, and ruled out any express willingness to undergo sacrifices in the interest of creditors of 1824 and 1825. Greece replied with thanks, and expressed its willingness to make available one-third of the revenue of the customs of Syros[158] — and this was finally an end to negotiations lasting 22 years. At the same time, on 17 March 1864, in London the treaty by which the Ionian Islands were united with Greece was also concluded, and by

---

Commission's conclusions were accepted by the Powers, and also had to be accepted by Greece, which Sir Wyse told Kondouriotis on 21 October.

[156] See *Livre Jaune* of 1866, pages 71 – 81, and also G. de Monicault, *Le Traité de Paris et ses suites* (1856 - 1871), pages 255 - 257.

[157] See *Livre Jaune*, page 73.

[158] See Comunicazione of Boudouris to Count de Gobineau (15/27 January 1865), *Livre Jaune*, page 76.

virtue of this treaty, the Powers undertook to pay annually to His Majesty George four thousand Pounds, each taken from the amount paid to them by the Greek treasury. These twelve thousand Pounds, said the treaty, were available to the King, in addition to the Civil List provided by state law.

And so, in 1865, the issue was in the following condition:

1) Against the Sixty Million Loan, that the guaranteeing Powers had served, completing the amortization in 1871 with a total expenditure of 100,392,833 Francs[159], Greece undertook to pay 900,000 Francs, one-third of which, however, returned to the king as a supplement to the Civil List.

2) The amount of 900,000 Francs was a minimum that the Powers had retained the right to increase when economic conditions of Greece would improve. This interpretation was expressed in a speech of Gladstone in the House of Commons, 22 March 1869. According to Gladstone, the provisional agreement of 1860 would not be considered even a treaty in the full sense, and it let the Powers be free to increase the amount claimed[160].

Provisional in theory, in practice the agreement acted as definitive: The Powers did not demand compliance with the condition that Greece should not commit any resources to satisfy the bondholders of 1824 and 1825, nor ever exercised the right to increase the yearly amount[161]. So, the situation was stabilized by the payment of an amount which was small in relation to the burden borne by the Powers, but nevertheless was disproportionate to the actual benefit that Greece obtained from the loan, consisting, as we know, only of redemption of Phthiotis and repayment of some previous smaller loans.

However, it remains a subtle question, i.e.: Are the 900,000 Francs currently paid each year paid as interest, amortization or both? The importance of the matter is clear: If the sum is paid as interest, it is true that we are paying 0.9% instead of 5%, but we will pay forever, or at least until new agreements are made.

---

[159] See Λιακόπουλον, *Εθνικά Δάνεια*, page 32.

[160] See Proceedings of the House of Commons in *The Times* of 23 March 1860 and a letter of *Economicus* to *The Times* of 10 November 1875.

[161] Except for a tentative one in 1892, about which I was informed by Platoukas, at the time director of the Public Debt Department.

The doubt is more than justified, since the agreements make no explicit mention of this aspect. In 1859, the Powers demanded simply the payment of the sum of 900,000 Francs, which at that time was considered sufficient, and the Greek Government merely enrolled in the budget the year after. The same speech of the King on 22 October 1859 in front of Parliament contains a hint to the ambiguity of the agreement: "It is well known that My Government, which worked so hard to keep the commitments of the nation towards the guarantor Powers, proposed them to regulate the issue of the loan in a way proportionate to the forces of the state. The Powers *for the present* required the annual payment of 900,000 Francs. My Government now requires the necessary approval to you, and then *will resume the negotiations for final settlement* of the debt issue, a necessary condition for economic reform and the restoration of public faith."[162]

The ambiguity of the agreement since then has generated confusion in the public; a committee of the Senate, among other questions asked to the Minister of Economy Koumoundouros, expressed the desire to know "if the payment of 1,005,120 Drachmas (900,000 Francs) will result in a decrease of remaining debt, and to what extent,"[163] but the minister said that "this is not easy to answer because the question is not yet solved." Then the commission asked to inspect at least the diplomatic documents, but the minister said again that the state's interest did not allow the publication of these documents for the time "because the issue was not yet fully defined."[164]

From the time of minister Koumoundouros' communications, nothing occurred that might clarify the issue, and the question is even more complicated now, because the treaty of 1859 was renewed in 1864 for five years, but later was never renewed again officially. Today, it seems to be tacitly renewed indefinitely, but there is not any text or any agreement stating that this should happen. It is no wonder that there are conflicting interpretations. The Greeks Dyobouniotis and Liakopoulos seem to regard it merely as amortization: The one in 1893 computed the remaining capital to

---

[162] *Πρακτικά Βουλής*, pages 4 – 5.

[163] *Πρακτικά Γερουσίας*, page 501.

[164] Report by senator Chatziskos in *Πρακτικά Γερουσίας*, page 494.

73,202,720 Francs[165], while the other considers the amount to be 66,002,720 Francs to 1st January 1900[166], but nobody indicates the source on which his calculations are based. A different opinion is that of French Stourm[167], but he commits a palpable error. According to him, the debt of Greece to France will be extinct in 2022, basing the calculation on 200,000 Francs paid every year to France; yet the sum actually paid is 300,000 Francs, because the French Government made the choice to donate 100,000 Francs to the Civil List of the King of Greece, and its voluntary act cannot go back on the shoulders of the Greek finances.

Wanting to get to the roots of the question, first I have tried in vain to gather information from the Division of Public Debt (Ministry of Economy) and by the Ministry of Foreign Affairs, and then I tried the office of the International Control. Here I was made aware that the question of the nature of the annual installment of 900,000 Francs is expressly defined in a *mémoire secret* (secret memorandum) dating back to 1859, whose contents are still unknown, but which should consider the sum as an amortization. There is evidence that this information is true in the public documents of the agreements of 1898. The Annexes of those agreements contain tables of the government debt, where the first column gives the total capital, and the second column gives the remainder at that date, under the title of *Sommes non amorties* (not amortized amounts). For the loan of the three Powers, the first column gives the correct value of 100,392,833 Francs, while the second item contains the simple word *mémoire* (to remember)[168].

We find ourselves in a position of not knowing how much money we owe, not unlike what happened eleven years ago to Mr. Law, who in his *Report on the present economical and financial position in Greece* declared that he could not complete the overview of the situation as related to the loan of the three Powers, as he had no way

---

[165] Page 33.

[166] *Δημόσιον Χρέος*, page 6 n. 1.

[167] *Le budget*, chapter XI. Services spéciaux du trésor, page 235 n. (edizione 1891). Anyway, it is to say that Stourm merely hints at the issue, talking about another question, a *service spécial* of public debt that existed in France before 1887.

[168] See *Livre Jaune* 1898 (Arrangement financier avec la Grèce) page 16.

B. The debt under the Bavarian dynasty

of knowing the data[169].

---

[169] Page 14, note 3. Law received a vehement but not exact answer by D. Georgiadis, see *La Grèce Economique et Financière en 1893* (Réponse à M. Law), page 58.

B.2. Bavarian loans and debts with the heirs of Othon

B.2.1 Bavarian loans

Sources of knowledge of the story are the study of Sicherer — in particular, diplomatic documents collected there in the appendix, the Acts of Parliament of 11 and 12 December 1880, where there is a remarkable speech by Kalligas[170], and some newspaper articles of 1880[171]. Finally, the archivist Trost in 1891 published some letters of king Ludwig I to his son Othon in which recur mentions of the Greek loans and of non-repayment.

The reason why the Bavarian loans were contracted was the delay in the third series of the Sixty Million Loan, of which we talked above. The Greek Government, which based all of its accounts on the Sixty Million Loan, at the beginning of 1835 found itself in a very worrisome situation, so H. M. King of Bavaria, "wishing to express the constant interest for the welfare of the Greek Nation and Monarchy which He does not cease to feel"[172] (as says the preface of the agreement of 8 June 1835), was pleased to offer one million Francs to 4%, to be repaid immediately upon delivery of the remainder of the Sixty Million Loan. This sympathy for Greece later created unpleasant consequences for King Ludwig: The loan was not repaid by the Greeks, and when Ludwig abdicated in 1848, the Bavarians held him responsible and loaded on him all of the financial consequences of the unfortunate agreement with Greece, claiming from him the satisfaction of the claims of the Treasury.

In 1836, the situation had not changed, and Ludwig returned to offer help with two loans — the one of a million Francs on 10 March, and the other of a million Bavarian Gulden (equivalent to slightly more than two million Francs) on 25 December, always to 4%. Shortly after the third series of the Sixty Million Loan was paid — minus the compound interest of the previous years on the first part of the loan and other liabilities of the budget — there was not enough to pay off the Bavarian debt, which came to the figure of 4,640,000 Drachmas. So, on 15 March 1838, it was necessary to agree that the Greek Government would extinguish the debt with one million within the current year, with a half-million in 1839, and then again

---

[170] Reproduced in *Μελέταις και Λόγοις*, vol. 2° page 445 – 451.

[171] *Αιώνος* of 1 and 9 August 1880, and *Εθνοφύλακος* 8 August 1880.

[172] See Sicherer, Appendix, page 3.

with instalments of one million over the next years. But it was immediately obvious that the conditions were too heavy, so the pact was revised, allowing Greece to pay only the first instalment of half a million, and the rest starting in 1840. This instalment was paid, and so three quarterly instalments in 1841 for another 750,000 Francs, but then it came time to pay the interest on the larger loan and repairs to Turkey, so it was agreed with Bavaria's that the remaining debt, 2,917,711 Francs, would be repaid in instalments of lesser amounts from then until 1847[173]. The first of these, 250,000 Francs, was paid, and then came the uprising of 3 September 1843, which, as it was animated by both the maturation of a sincere desire to establish the Constitution and by the accumulated hatred towards the Government of Bavaria, obviously had consequences also on the question of the Bavarian loan. The political history of Greece was kept out of this book, in which I wanted to acknowledge openly the many mistakes made by our country, but now is the time to digress a moment and to consider that the hatred towards the Government of Bavaria in that time was longer justified, after the squandering of resources by the regency, the scandals in the military administration and in any other branch of the government, where being a Bavarian descendant was much more important than merit, and where the German had become a semi-official language. Moreover, the devastating consequences of the attempt to make Greece Bavarian-like were so obvious that they were forecast even in some writings of king Ludwig himself, who in 1833 observed that "the Greeks needed to become Greeks and not to germanise," and to his son, on the verge of becoming an adult, remembered "that the Greeks do not need to be bavarized, but to be governed in the spirit of their nation."

As a result of anti-Bavarian feelings, then it happened that while the delays of payments of the Sixty Million Loan were always considered interim measures due to reasons of force majeure, the Bavarian loan was put into question regarding its very legitimacy. After a spirited debate, which was owed mainly to the pen of Levidos, editor of the newspaper *Elpis*, the public opinion forced the parliament to vote on a measure whose main provisions were, first, that the government, under the responsibility of the Council of Ministers, should take into consideration all documents exchanged between the Court of Bavaria and the London Council of the three

---

[173] Precisely, 250.000 Francs in 1842 and 1843, 500.000 from 1844 to 1846 and 417.711 in 1847.

Great Powers regarding the establishment of the Kingdom of Greece, and should submit to the Parliament before the next session a detailed report of each element clarifying the financial situation that was found in the documentation. Then, the Parliament would have the task of examining the resulting financial position and dealing with Bavaria's claims against Greece through diplomatic channels and through the mediation of the Protecting Powers.

The decision of the Parliament mentioned the commitments that Bavaria had taken with the protocols of London on 26 April 1832 regarding the royal financial endowment, the board of regents, and the accompaniment of the prince and the army into Greece, trying to justify the failure to service the loan with the argument of not complying with those commitments by Bavaria. It also tried to appeal to quirky topics, such as that the stipulation of the loan had not been published in the Official Gazette, and many others that do not deserve discussion.

But on the basis of the protocols, it was not possible to argue that Greece was exempted from paying fees to the ordinary civil and military officials on its service, even when Bavaria had pledged to continue to pay them the salary they were receiving at home; and the issue of 1843, repeated by one of our MP, deputy Dimitriadis, yet in 1880, that the cost of the regency was to be borne entirely by Ludwig, was not serious from a legal standpoint, because the regency was not employed by Ludwig, but was the sovereign of a state that was independent, and which therefore answered the acts of his government.

The public opinion of the time considered valid these arguments, claiming a nonexistent legal liability from the real moral responsibility that Ludwig bore for his poor choices, and that the regency bore for its insane administration. There are confusions which happen to everyone, but that should not be allowed to politicians and parliaments; and instead the measure voted in 1843 is a legal monster, as also Kalligas[174] observed.

Bavaria, however, did not protest immediately. Only two years later, the Bavarian ambassador Gesser was to express grievances for deferred payments and for non-budgeting the amount of debt, but Kolettis answered simply by sending the report on the financial

---

[174] See *Μελέταις και Λόγοις*, page 451.

position of Metaxas[175], about which we talked. The answer, although legally inconsistent, grasped the essence of the matter, so that for fourteen years the issue was hardly spoken of; only in 1852, when the rumour spread that the debt of Sixty Million would be settled, did Bavaria remember its rights through a communication of its ambassador, Baron von Perglas. But on 11 September 1859, an unexpected communication from the Bavarian Government came to the Greek one, reporting to have transferred its credits from Greece to its former king Ludwig, in compensation for the deposition of 1849 and as reimbursement of the costs he personally incurred for the erection of many of the monuments that adorn the city of Munich, and demanded the liquidation of capital and interest on the amount of 1,933,333 Gulden and 20 Kreuzer[176].

King Othon put forth all of his effort to get the possibility of adjusting the matter by enrolling the sum of one million into the budget accepted by the government. Assuring himself the consent of some ministers, he decided to preside personally over a cabinet meeting in which he tried to persuade the others even by starvation, in a meeting that lasted eight hours in a summer day. But the ministers Zaimis and Rallis exercised the most stubborn opposition, and the king was obliged to hand it over[177]. Then the Greek Government refused to make any step forward in the matter, responding to Bavaria that the settlement of the Sixty Million loan was a priority, and that the other loans would be discussed only afterward.

Thus, the claims of Bavaria seemed buried once and for all, when in 1880 intervened Bismarck, who had meanwhile ascertained that Greece had recognized his debts, and who used to practice the policy of making personal services to the ancient royal families of German states now included the Germanic Empire. Through the German ambassador von Radowitz, the Iron Chancellor demanded the settlement of claims of the heirs of Ludwig, having good arguments because at that time, Greece was awaiting the execution of the clauses of the Treaty of Berlin of 1878 and could not invoke the usual topics to gain time. The government knew that it had to submit

---

[175] See Sicherer, Appendice, page 38.

[176] In Francs about the double (Editor's note).

[177] Zaimis told this story in an article of *Ethnofylax* on 8 August 1880.

to the game, and sent to Germany the jurist Stephanos Streit, who, through shrewd negotiations, managed to settle the claim of 5,600,000 Francs with a one-off payment of 2,600,000 Francs to Prince Ferdinand of Bavaria. This transaction was ratified by Parliament on 14 December 1880, and the Bavarian debt issue was shelved.

B.2.2 *Debt to the heirs of King Othon*

Sources for this story are the agreement of 28 October 1868 with the heirs of Othon and parliamentary acts[178]. The debt in question is often confused with the former one, because in both cases, the Greek nation had the Wittelsbach family as a counterpart. But the two debts were of an entirely different nature, because the first, as we know, was the result of the advances granted by King Ludwig, while the second originated from expenditures made by the private cash of King Othon for the construction of royal palaces, for their gardens, for the Royal Pharmacy which now houses the Ministry of War, for the construction of the Hippodrome, and from numerous other expenses incurred by the late king for the maintenance of equipment and real estate, as well as for integration of the Civil List. The total until the day of the deposition of Othon in 1862 was estimated to be four million by some, and even seven-and-a-half[179] by others. The National Assembly challenged the very legitimacy of the claim of the king, without arriving at any conclusion, although four solutions were taken into consideration: Confiscating the property of Othon; an interpretation that considered it as national estate; another interpretation that kings have no right to private property; and finally redemption. The Athenians lawyers officially stated that they believed Othon not to have property rights, and unofficially expressed the opinion that he was not entitled to compensation.

The representatives of the three Powers suggested that the debt to King Othon would be mentioned in the treaty that would assign the Ionian Islands to Greece in 1864. This did not happen, but the Minister Trikoupis failed to prevent the Powers from officially requiring the recognition of debt, for which King Othon had immediately taken a strongly purposeful initiative. Shortly after the death of the king, on 8 July 1868, the government signed an agreement with his heirs, including Queen Amalia, acknowledging

---

[178] Ordinary Session of 1868, pages 507 - 513.
[179] See Valassopoulos, page 511.

them a credit of 4,500,000 Francs[180]. According to the agreement, Greece would pay the debt "as speedily, and if possible within eight years," but then it was paid a little at a time[181], and I was informed amicably by the current director of the Public Debt, Miliotis, that it will be terminated by the end of 1908.

---

[180] See Liakopoulos page 102-104. The agreement was ratified by the Parlamento on 11 November, with 92 votes against 18.

[181] The residue debt amount was 2.536.476 franchi in 1893, in 1898 was 1.546.232, in 1902 was 952.977 and in 1903 it was 789.405.

B.3. Domestic debt and pensions

B.3.1. Domestic debt

The domestic debt, in the exact sense of the word, shrinks to very little, because beyond the compensation due to the Nautical Islands, which will be discussed separately, and beyond a small advance of the National Bank, the internal debt consisted solely of the repayment of some debts assumed by the Provisional Government and in the repayment of the Capital of the first National Bank. These refunds actually occurred, so that the total sum of 158,148 Drachmas in 1833 dropped to 1,460 in 1842. After 1843, the amount increased a bit, and arrived to the sum of 26,870 Drachmas, as a result of obligations undertaken in the past.

B.3.2. Pensions

Pensions, in the proper sense of the word, did not exist because the early retirement benefits were instituted in 1852. Under the heading of pensions were enrolled certain financial rewards and some compensations that were considered right, which were paid after the Independence War. These so-called pensions were divided into five classes, and were paid:

1) to *veterans*, to whom treatments were recognized by *ad personam* decree. In the budget of 1845[182], there were 396, for a total of 7,305 Drachmas.

2) to the *widows and orphans* of men who had given extraordinary contributions to the service of the Fatherland. In 1845, there were 1,788 pensions of this class, for a total of 19,064 Drachmas. The highest pensions were those paid to Chrisoula Botzaris (225 Drachmas per month), to the orphans of Kolokotronis and Kaiaiskakis (120 and 106 Drachmas), and the family Diligiannis (90 Drachmas). Other pensions were insignificant.

3) to *Phalanx veterans*: there were a dozen or so former members

---

[182] I prefer to refer to the budget of 1845 for three reasons: because it was the first since the promulgation of the Constitution, because it contains a number of explanatory notes of its items, and because it was under the control of the three Protecting Powers, so that it gives details and information that are not present in any of the other budgets.

of the Phalanx that a royal decree had considered worthy of a special contribution; in 1845, they were 9 and received 375 Drachmas per month.

4) to the *holders of ancient rights*. These subsidies were paid to creditors of the provisional government, which had sacrificed entire estates to the nation. Among these was, before all, the family Zaimis, who received a monthly subsidy of 555 Drachmas; and then many families of Nautical Islands: Οικονόμου (552 Drachmas), Σαχτούρη (360), Αναργύρου (332), Μπουδούρη (318), Μπόταση (318). The large number of families of the Nautical Islands receiving these subsidies, compared to many others who did not receive anything (such as the Kondouriotis), was one of the reasons that led to the settlement of the claims of the Nautical Islands with the Law of 1853, which will be discussed in the last chapter. In 1845, the recipients of this type of grant were 111 in total, with an expense of 9,304 Drachmas per month[183].

5) as *dowries to the orphans of men who distinguished themselves in war*. Up to 1844 dowries were arranged with royal decrees for 150,950 Drachmas[184], but in fact, 73,595 were not paid, and 10,020 were cancelled, so that this expenditure consisted of 67,335 Drachmas paid to 522 persons. But since it was established that dowries of more than 200 Drachmas would be paid through the allotment of land, the budget would register under this item only 3,000 Drachmas. The only significant dowry was the one given to the daughter of I. Kriezis, of 5005 Drachmas[185].

In all, the spending for these five classes of pensions grew from 172,515 Drachmas in 1833 to an average of 400,000 in a few years[186]. As also recognized by About's book, it was not a hyperbolic

---

[183] Precisely, there were 27 persons who received from 80 to 555 Drachmas monthly, 6 between 55 and 70, 12 between 34 and 50, 16 between 20 and 30 and 50 between 6 and 15.

[184] Precisely, in 1833 dr. 3.800, in 1834 dr. 35.140, in 1835 dr. 51.150, in 1836 dr. 27.140 and until 1844 other 33,720.

[185] Others, however, were awarded with separate special measures, such as the dowry given to the Karaisakis' daughter to marry Notaras, and to the daughter of Kondouriotis, who married Kondostavlos.

[186] For example, 239.329 Drachmas in were spent in 1834, 357.976 in 1839, and 426.031 in 1842. The sum dropped to 377.495 in 1843

figure, considering how many people were completely ruined after the Independence, and considering the dire economic situation and the great difficulties which encountered anyone trying to find a job.

But to these pensions, paid by way of indemnity or contribution, were to be added many more, provided by different ministries:

from the Ministry of the War, Drs 579,095.01 (481,763.30 of which to the Phalanx, and 97,331.76 for military pensions not further described);

Ministry of the Navy, forty pensions for 9,784.80 Drachmas;

Ministry of Education, 71,103 Drachmas in ecclesiastical pensions to compensate the revenue of land devolved to the state;

Ministry of Justice, 2,040 Drachmas;

Ministry of Foreign Affairs, 23,994 Drachmas in civil pensions, not to mention 75,000 in other aid.

In all, then, were 686,016 Drachmas, which, added to the first 400,000, brought the burden for the state to over one million — a figure disproportionate to the overall public spending, which then was burdened for another substantial sum on account of the wages paid to certain public officials who were entitled to get them only by the services, sometimes at all imaginary, provided by their fathers to the cause of Independence. Also noteworthy is the finding that over the years and until the present time, this number of people who asked the state for rewards for the deeds of their ancestors has increased instead of decreasing. Nowadays, one could suspect that the only ones who refrain from these requirements are the descendants of those who have sacrificed real life or wealth for the nation.

To this million are to be added more than 75,000 Drachmas paid in subsidies by the Ministry of Foreign Affairs; and with regard to the spending of ministries in general, that is what the Minister of the Navy Konstantinos Kanaris wrote at the time[187]: "We have four hundred officers, three hundred and six of which are not in active service. For these officers kept available we spend 264,492 Drachmas annually, an amount equal to that spent for the entire staff of the Navy on active duty, and increasing from year to year. However, almost all officers are people to whom the nation owes its

---

and then was stabilized to about 400.000 Drachmas per year.

[187] Annotation of 26 April 1846 to the budget of 1845, whose approval was pending, pages 81-85.

freedom and independence"[188].

In this context, the establishment of the *Phalanx* gave rise to numerous controversies. It had a dual purpose, openly mentioned by royal decree, that instituted it on 18/30 September 1834: "The Phalanx is created to give an expression of royal favour and of gratitude of the Fatherland to the brave men, which gave their services as leaders of their comrades in the fight for Greek Independence, and to give them the opportunity to respond to the call of the king and to make new services." Thus conceived, the Phalanx was perfectly justified, and could prove useful to the nation. But in fact, it was not organized with judgement, nor ever made services that are worth mentioning.

In the Phalanx were enlisted 900 officers who had been *leaders of their comrades in the fight* only in their imaginations, and who constituted an hypertrophic staff costing one million a year. The problem was immediately visible with such evidence, so that in 1838 a law was established that members of the phalanx who would not agree to move to the provinces where there was need of their service would be put to rest with a liquidation equivalent to the amount of their fees, paid by the allotment of national lands. The number of members of the phalanx fell from 900 to 350, and the expenditure from one million to 400,000 Drachmas, and to members who had resigned were granted vouchers for the allocation of national land for a total value of over five million[189]. But many among those who had resigned did not give sufficient attention to redeem the vouchers, but instead sold them to 25 or 30% of their value, and squandered the cash, thereby falling rapidly into poverty[190]. Then, instead of bearing

---

[188] Kanaris added that "The veterans company founded in 1833 with partially disabled sailors includes 46 men and involves the expenditure of 24,142 Drachmas per year."

[189] Precisely, in 1838 3.719.902 Drachmas, in 1839 697.520, in 1840 199.320, in 1841 150.960, in 1842 110.544 and in 1843 615.393 for a total amount of 5.493.639 Drachmas. See the report by Metaxas, page LI.

[190] The cause of the members of the Phalanx was advocated by Senator Rigas Palamidis in the session of 8 October 1856. Unscrupulous as he was about economic matters, he exposed to the Senate the injustices of which the people of the Phalanx had been the victim, though he forgot the chapter on their abuse. See also the

the consequences of their little careful life policy, some resorted to the powerful patronage at their disposal to be re-enrolled in the Phalanx, which surprisingly took place, and that raised its annual cost to half a million[191]. Other amounts were spent also in purchasing land vouchers from those members of the Phalanx who had kept them in their hands.

In the following years, the staff of the Phalanx was reduced to 240 men, until it was dissolved by an Act of 12 October 1856 on "retirement and financial endowment of the Phalanx effectives," which converted the salaries of effective members into retirement pensions paid by the Ministry of War.

And that is all concerning the pensions paid until the year 1852. After that year, it was recognized that a pension system was necessary for the staff of the Army, the Navy, and the Civil Service, and a number of laws abrogated the old five classes of pensions by reforming the criteria of their budgeting. The budget of 1862, the last under the dynasty of Bavaria, counted the debt service to 2,848,889 Drachmas for pensions shown in this table[192]:

---

novel *Thanos Vlekas* by Kalligas at page 137.

[191] See about this issue the report of the French ambassador Guerin, reproduced in Leconte, pages 155-166.

[192] Sums do not match exactly, due to misprints in the text (Editor's note).

Pensions	Persons	Expense	Total expense
Army			
Old pensions from 1834	1780	559.998	961.550
New from 1852			
Demobilization of the Phalanx	323	313.782	
Increases		25.000	
20% increase to the Phalanx		62.756	
Navy			
Old from 1834	592	146.658	438.046
New from 1853			
Demobilization bonuses	202	221.990	
Increases		25.000	
20% increase to demobilized		44.394	
Ecclesiastical pensions			
Old from 1834	28		14.049
Civil pensions			
Old from 1834	31		52.928
New from 1855			
Integration of the Civil Service Pension Cash[193]			100.000
Total			*1.566.523*

Tab. 9

With this we enter into the story of an era that is no longer that of the original foundation of the Greek state, and in which pensions are paid as a result of services more or less really given. An echo of the original era is still felt in the laws of February 1859, which stipulated that "the period of service giving right to a pension entitlement is reduced to 15 years for widows and orphans of officers who served and fell in the fight for the homeland, or in the fight for the establishment of the Constitution." This was a criterion that the Interpretative Commission of the Parliament judged "charitable and just, for it is favourable to families of men who knew only the pain of the struggle, and did not receive any personal satisfaction from the strain to which they underwent for the freedom of the nation."[194]

---

[193] The civilian pension cash was fueled by deductions from salaries, and supplemented annually with state aid.

[194] See meeting of 16 December 1858, page 188, Proceedings of 1858-1859.

B.4. Debt to the Nautical Islands

The services rendered to the nation by the three islands of Hydra, Spetses, and Psara, which bore almost the entire burden of the war at sea and thus were then called Nautical Islands (ναυτικάι νήσοι), are well known. Also well known are the great financial sacrifices with which those islands were able to cover the operating costs of the excellent fleet they had armed.

The importance of the sacrifices can be appreciated even more, considering that the three small islands contributed to the costs of the war with 20 million old Drachmas, or 18 million new ones, against the remaining budget that totalled 37,800,000 Drachmas, of which 22 million and a half were from domestic resources, and 15,300,000 from foreign borrowing[195]. These contributions were conferred by the many affluent families existing in the Nautical Islands at the time — especially by the Kondouriotis — while in the rest of Greece, the financial contributions came from all classes of the population. According to official data[196], the contribution of Kondouriotis amounted to 2,141,806 Drachmas — an immense figure, given the value of money at that time. This was comparable to ten million in 1904, and otherwise represented the entire wealth of the family. Other significant contributions came from the Boudouridis and Tombazidis of Hydra (764,114 and 559,170 Drachmas), by the Anargiri, Botasis and Mexis of Spetses (609,606, 453,530 and 430,606 Drachmas), by the Apostoloi and Kotzadis of Psara (495,570 and 448,133 Drachmas).

The attitude of the Kondouriotis family was considered by many to be a factor in the success of the Independence War. Mendelssohn-Bartholdy reports some words of Lazaros Kondouriotis: "I spent thirty years struggling to accumulate wealth, and now I consider myself lucky because I can spend it on the liberation of the homeland. And I am convinced that the whole population of Hydra share my feelings, and even if you see others hesitate to spend, do

---

[195] The long history of Independence by Paparrigopoulos gives account of the financial aspects of the contribution of the Nautical Islands. Instead, Andreas Orlandos, who wrote a work in two volumes on the war on the sea, almost does not speak at all of the financial aspect.

[196] Official Journal of 30 July 1856.

not worry: I am able to finance by myself throughout the war at sea."[197]

The extraordinary services rendered by the islands were always recognized by the Greek Government, which also gave some compensation during the war, and afterward acknowledged the islands' requests as valid. Accepting the uncertain sources as good, and considering that the islands were also compensated by the spoils of war and the capture of the Turkish ships, the islands may have received 1,400,000 Drachmas during the war[198].

Instead, a final balance of the sacrifices borne by Peloponnese and mainland Greece has never been reached. There were repeated attempts to settle the question, on which a committee chaired by Rigas Palamidis worked for a long time, but the public opinion was always suspicious about the basis of the claims of other regions, while considering it a duty to satisfy the demands of the islands[199]. The view that the rest of Greece (and especially Peloponnese) had not given the economic contributions due dates from the time of Independence, and for example is expressed in a letter written by Kolokotronis to Mexis and other notables of Spetses on 18 October 1822: "By us here the people of rank do not take example from you, do not spend their own money, but appropriate the Fatherland's resources, and then get rebels to defend themselves, and this is a

---

[197] Page 279 of the Greek translation, Vol. 1.

[198] Already in 1823, the islands acquired (See Αν. Ορλάνδου, Ναυτικά vol. 1° page 440) 26.000 Piastres by a collection in the Peloponnese, 36.000 by contributions of the towns of Corinth, Kalavryta, Nauplia and Vostitza (later named Aigion), 12.518 by private additions to those contributions, and 46.338 from the sale of national land, for a total of 121.148 piastre. According to the recollection of Vice-Admiral Nikodemos (see Paparrigopoulos, page 791), it is possible that in 1824 Psara already received 120.000 piastre, Spetses 160.000 and Idra 240.000, plus 94.000 Piastres more from the 1824 loan (Idra 47.000, Spetses 32.000 and Psara 15.000). Finally, after the capture of Corinth, the islands received 35,000 Piastres in cash, with part of the of the booty in jewels, and an approximate value of 213,000 plates according to Andreas Orlandos, or of 800,000, according to others.

[199] See Paparrigopoulos, page 781.

source of extreme bad luck, and we run the risk of losing."[200] In a letter written by a Greek in Leghorn to Romas[201], we read that "those of the Morea seem all vanished, and say they have no money, and have underwritten willingly only a few bonds."

In fact, even in Peloponnese resources were gathered, as we saw in the first chapter, and also in Peloponnese there were families who risked fortunes (as the Diligiannis did), which, according to a reliable source, may claim the credit of 1,700,000 Piastres. We know, moreover, that this controversial issue is part of the old wounds of our history.

The story of the recognition of obligations to the Nautical Islands went on for a long time. The islands demanded recognition of their right to compensation in the National Assembly at Astros on 14 April 1823, which allowed it[202], though not without a long discussion. Shortly afterward, the Assembly of Epidaurus decided to recognize charges incurred by the islands in the period between 1823 and 1826 as public debt[203]. Then, in front of the fourth National Assembly, the government proposed to grant some small interim compensation to the three islands: 147,000 Drachmas to Hydra, 63,000 to Spetses, and 90,000 to Psara. But after the assassination of Kapodistrias, the issue was quelled at long, causing riots in 1838 in Hydra (though these were also a result of the earthquake that devastated the island). However, since the country shared the feeling of being beholden to the Nautical Islands, pensions were granted to many families, as we have seen, and especially to those who were able to produce indisputable documents. The diversity of treatments finally forced the state to face the problem of equity among the beneficiaries, and the matter was cleared up by an Act of 22 January 1853[204] and a royal decree of 12 July 1856, which adjusted the credit

---

[200] The language of the letter of the general, who was a former robber, is folksy: "Οι άρχοντές μας δεν παραδειγματίζονται εις σας, να εξοδεύσουν από τα ιδικά των, αλλά σφετερίζονται τα της πατρίδος και προς διαφέντευσίν των στασιάζουν και προξενείται εκ τούτου εσχάτη δυστυχία και κινδυνεύομεν να χαθώμεν" (Editor's note).

[201] *Αρχείον Ρώμα*, page 65.

[202] See Μάμουκαν, vol. 3° pages 22 - 24.

[203] See Μάμουκαν, vol. 4° pages 119.

[204] See Proceedings of the Lower House (pages 169 - 180, 15

of the islands by 20 million old Drachmas, against which an annual 1% interest, or 200,000 Drachmas, was paid.

A table attached to the decree of 1856 presents the following summary of the credit of the three islands:

Hydra		
For arming and equipment of ships		2.967.948
For the use of ships in war		2.773.968
For anticipations to the treasury		1.187.586
For reparations of ships		1.293.108
For public collections and payments during the war		1.642.166
For expences made by the community	282.224	135.224
whose already paid back by the Government	-147.000	
TOTAL Hydra		*10.000.000*
Spetses		
For arming and equipment of ships		2.867.512
For the use of ships in war		2.138.202
For anticipations to the treasury		173.800
For expences made by the community	480.486	390.486
whose already paid back by the Government	-90.000	
TOTAL Spetses		*5.570.000*
Psara		
For arming and equipment of ships		2.276.408
For the use of ships in war		1.341.522
For anticipations to the treasury		578.638
For expences made by the community	296.432	233.432
whose already paid back by the Government	-63.000	
TOTAL Psara		*4.430.000*
GENERAL TOTAL		*20.000.000*

Tab. 10

This provisional settlement of the issue lasted from that time until the present year of 1904, although it is not satisfactory, because on one hand the recognition of an interest of 1% can hardly be considered sufficient to meet the nation's commitments, and secondly, because as the time went by, the original beneficiaries have increasingly sold their titles to third parties, so the day is not far when the entire amount of the sum will be paid to people who have no substantive right to the gratitude of the nation. The latter fact has forced us to revisit the issue by the Act of 16 June 1904, which

---

December 1852) and of the Senate (pages 156 - 162, 14 January 1853), especially the report of senator Magginas, who had been a member of two commissions on the issue.

provides that entitled persons will receive registered or bearer bonds to 1% for a total capital of 18 million, which will be awarded on the basis of payments made until the present time. To allow the amortization of the debt, plus interest, will be registered in the budget each year the sum of 20,000 Drachmas intended to pay off bonds randomly selected, and then the sinking fund will be increased by interest on extinct bonds. In addition, the new bonds will be accepted at par for the renewal of public debt shares subscribed by holders, and for the purchase of real estate of the state or of church. And finally, those who will not require the new bonds within five years will forfeit their right.

These measures of the current year have not received a very favourable reception. Some newspapers have insisted that after fifty years, it would be worthwhile to recognize the new bonds only for the descendants of those who had original rights to compensations, and instead, because the original rights were mostly sold at low prices, the result of the law is nothing more than to reward the cleverness of speculators. This is a consideration not without grounds, but I could verify that this year, a great number of families whose original titles of right had never been defeated have benefited from the law. Thus, as it was necessary that the issue would receive a final settlement, any further procrastination would only increase the injustice of the outcome.

If we wish to criticize the details of the law, there would certainly be much to say: The law was made in haste without a thorough preliminary study, and therefore contains elements of difficult application, which a decree attempted to remedy but resulted in making the matter even worse. Suffice it to say that while the law provided that the new bonds were to be delivered against the only documentation of payments previously received, the decree requires of persons entitled the full presentation of their qualifications.

Conclusion of the editor (March 2012)

At this point, Andreadis summarized in another table the numbers now well known, and introduced with few words the rest of the narrative — which, however, was never written.

The story, in brief, is this. For the next twenty years following the agreements of 1878, Greece adopted a political system similar to a bipolar one, in which Trikoupis alternated in power several times with Diligiannis. Trikoupis was a Westernizing reformer, anxious to consolidate Greece and develop it economically and politically, whereas Diligiannis, the scion of a family of Peloponnesian notables, was a champion of "Great Greece," a proponent of irredentist adventures and unable to go beyond the simple negation of Trikoupis' reforms. Thus, he declared expressly that its policy was being against anything that Trikoupis was favourable.

With the support of business and merchant classes, Trikoupis engaged in a not entirely unsuccessful effort to develop the country's economy. We know that before 1878, it had been impossible for Greece to raise funds in the international market; after the agreement of that year for the settlement of old debts, Trikoupis's program was financed by borrowing abroad and by increasing the tax revenue through a more rigorous tax collection, raising the tax burden mainly through indirect taxes, the increase of customs duties, and the exploitation of state monopolies, such as salt and matches. The agreements for the settlement of old debts, coupled with Trikoupis's moderation, inspired some confidence in foreign investors, and between 1879 and 1890 six contracts were signed for foreign loans with a nominal value of 630 million Drachmas, although the required interest, given that Greece was not yet considered entirely reliable, was 30%, resulting in a huge weight of interests in the state budget: Around 1887, 40% of the annual budget was allocated to repay interest and amortization.

Between 1880 and 1890, modest economic progress was recorded, and Greece was able to build a minimal rail and telegraph network; the total tonnage of steam ships flying the Greek flag went from 8241 tons in 1821 to 144,975 in 1895. Wealthy Greeks, often residing abroad, began to acquire a large number of old steam ships equipped with sailors of their islands and giving birth to a twentieth-century tradition in which Greece would have one the largest commercial fleets in the world. Many of the positive results obtained by Trikoupis, however, were demolished by the policy of Diligiannis and his demagogic exploitation of Greek irredentism. When, for example, Bulgaria annexed Eastern Rumelia in 1885, Greece called for territorial compensation, and Diligiannis ordered a general mobilization. However, the following year, after the imposition of the blockade by the Powers, Greece was forced to demobilize. The hasty mobilization proclaimed by Diligiannis had only resulted in a huge cost to the public finance that weighed on the next government of Trikoupis, who, in an attempt to bring order to the finances of the country and to reconstruct its international economic credibility, was forced to increase taxes again and thus to restore the strength of the demagogic populism of Diligiannis.

During the last Trikoupis Government (1892-95), the Greek financial situation became desperate. The collapse of the price of raisins on the international market revealed the essential fragility of an economy based almost exclusively on a very limited number of exported goods. The declining value of the Drachma caused the growth of interest on foreign debts that were paid in gold, and came to absorb up to half of the total revenues of the state. In 1893, the year of greatest crisis, imports reached 119,306,000 Francs, while exports did not surpass 82,261,000 Francs. Trikoupis was forced to declare a default, reducing interest payments on foreign loans by 70%, while revenue for the repayment of the debts was channelled directly into state coffers. This was followed by the international collapse of Greek credit, as evidenced by the fact that coupons to 5% of the loan of 1881, at the beginning of 1883 were worth 76 percent of nominal value, and in December of that year had fallen to 30%.

The economic difficulties associated with the financial crash of 1893 and the austerity measures imposed by Trikoupis made Diligiannis's victory in the next election in 1895 almost inevitable. Trikoupis consequently retired to Paris, where he died the following year, saving himself from witnessing the humiliating defeat of Greece by the Turks in 1897. The great crisis of that year originated with one of the recurrent Cretan insurrections, having broken out in 1895. The rebels were supported by the radical nationalist *Ethniki Eteria*, or National Society, although at first, Diligiannis refused the official backing of the government, in view of the fact that the Powers had sent a deterrence fleet in the island.

But in early 1897, giving way to popular interventionism and to King George's enthusiasm for the annexation of the island, Diligiannis sent ships and troops into Crete. After rejecting a proposal of autonomy of the island under the Ottoman sovereignty in March of 1897, and encouraged by the inability of the Powers to take concerted action to cool the crisis, Diligiannis ordered general mobilization. In the following month, the hostilities broke out in Thessaly, but the Greek army was unable to resist the invigorated Turkish one, and after a month suffered a final overwhelming defeat. The contrast between the ambitions and the modest military possibilities of Greece were demonstrated quite clearly: It was evident that Greece alone could never fight against the Ottoman Empire and hope to win.

Although Greece had suffered a military defeat, the terms of the peace treaty were relatively mild, thanks to the influence of the Powers, which, at least on this occasion, proved to be benign. Greece was forced to pay a war indemnity of four million Turkish liras and to give a series of insignificant border adjustments. But the most humiliating arrangement of the peace treaty was the establishment of the International Financial Control Commission, Διεθνής Οικονομικός Έλεγχος or ΔΟΕ, with British, French, Russian, German, Austro-Hungarian and Italian representatives, who were in charge of supervising the payment of interest on large external debts and who confiscated revenues from state monopolies of salt, kerosene, matches, and playing cards, as well as from the duties on tobacco and cigarette paper, in addition to the stamp duties and taxes collected by the customs of Piraeus Harbour, the biggest in the Kingdom[205].

The commission exercised its duties until the First World War, forcing Greece to comply with the conditions imposed. Then it had a marginal advisory role, but also survived the Second World War, after which the British Foreign Office considered it useless and advised its dismantling in the early '60s, but the consent of all parties for the termination took place only in 1978.

Do we need a category of interpretation?

A newspaper article of last February, signed by Paul Krugman and analyzing the present recession, assigned responsibility of it to the new kind of *gold standard* established by the strength and stability of the single European currency, and has challenged the German interpretation of the present European economic crisis, an interpretation that overstates the role of the government's fiscal irresponsibility, noting that "this view seems to adapt to Greece, but

---

[205] For this synthesis of the story between 1878 and 1897, see Clogg, pages 91-94 (Editor's note).

to no other country."[206]

Greece today, as yesterday, did something special compared to all other countries of this world: It has come to find itself in an irreparable financial situation, which however could be avoided through a rational political decision taken in time, while the financial catastrophes of other countries are determined by a complex web of relationships and social factors, in which there is no way to recognize an individual and identifiable unit to which it makes sense to attribute an exclusive responsibility for the events (unless you have recourse to the repertoire of conspiracy theories spreading every were about the responsibilities of the open and hidden world financial elite). In Greece, today as yesterday, it happened that the Government pro tempore wanted and made a conscious decision to reach a level of debt that the real economy cannot withstand. And worse today than yesterday, because at the time of the Sixty Million Loan it was Europe that played its game on the skin of a barely known Greece; the Governments of the Powers, as we have seen, pleased the Philhellenism of opinion public together with the rapacity of the investment banks, showing belief in the possibility of a rapid economic development of the Arcadian Mediterranean garden on which Europe projected its dreams and its domestic political frustrations at the time of Restoration. By recalling his departure in 1822, one of the philhellenic authors cited by Andreadis, the sincere Jourdain who had given credence to the financial alchemy of the Knights of Rhodes, said: "Many of my travel companions were going, like me, to lend their arms, that out Fatherland did not want any more, to the cause of humanity."[207]

However, it would be wrong to imagine that the Greek society of the time of Independence was literally naïf and primitive; on the contrary, just the philhellenic chronicles of nineteenth century show us a picture much more complex than what one would expect. Among the authors quoted by Andreadis, the accurate Finlay tells us in detail how the Greek Risorgimento had its roots in the formation of a culturally better-equipped society that occurred when the echo from the French Revolution was also felt in the Ottoman domains, and gives us a great deal of interesting information about the philhellenic myth of the noble Greek savage and about its falsity:

---

[206] Paul Krugman, "La vera malattia che piega l'Europa", *La Repubblica*, 28 February 2012.

[207] Jourdain, *Mémoires*, page 3.

Degraded as the condition of the Greeks was politically, it is probable that a larger proportion could read and write than among any other Christian race in Europe. The Greeks of every class have always set a higher value on a knowledge of letters than any other people. They have a national tendency to pedantism. At the commencement of this century the effects of the French Revolution were strongly felt in Greece. Classic history was studied; classic names were revived; Athenian liberty became a theme of conversation among men; Spartan virtue was spoken of by women; literature was cultivated with enthusiasm as a step to revolution.[208]

The observation is effective to correct the idea of a naive society: Pedantry is a disease of old age, not youth. And the most interesting evidence of the non-naiveté of the Greeks of the time comes as we learn from Finlay that in Greece arrived from Europe even some missionaries armed with the ambition to teach Greeks and civilize them, and who were frustrated in their expectations because they did not find the situation they had presumptuously imagined:

The state of education explains the failure of the missionaries sent from Europe and America to improve the religious ideas of the Greeks. In theological learning these missionaries were always inferior to many of the Greek clergy; in classical knowledge they were as much inferior to many lay teachers. During the period of destitution which succeeded the cessation of hostilities with the Turks, they were welcomed as teachers of elementary schools, and they were popular for a time, because they gave both instruction and books gratis; but, in order to make their schools of any use, they were obliged to employ Greeks as teachers.[209]

The journalist About, quite perfunctory but effective, gives us eloquent snapshots representing Greece twenty years later, which had a public opinion that was at all aware of things in the world:

According to them [the Greeks], all the events of Europe have Greece as their center and aim. If England makes a world exhibition it is to highlight the products of Greece, if France has a revolution is to provide interesting articles to newspapers in Athens, and if the Emperor Nicolas covets Constantinople is to give it as a homage to King Othon.[210]

---

[208] Finlay, *History of the Greek Revolution*, vol. 1°, page 20

[209] Finlay, *History of the Greek Revolution*, vol. 1°, page 19

[210] About, *La Grèce contemporaine*, page 53.

> Men are on the village square, occupied to settle the destinies of Europe, while women are in the fields, with a pick in hand and a child on their back. [211]

About, a champion of the simplistic belief in national character from which we would like to keep totally far away, presents things in farce, but it remains true that nineteenth-century Greece had an image of itself as an European country, and had the ability to participate in political and cultural public discourse of the time.

And that is why, because Greece is a European partner, it still seems reasonable and making sense imputing to it the guilt of its financial troubles, of infidelity to partners and creditors, of the inability to administer its own resources and the consequences of its decisions. And so, even if it is true that the decision to contract the Sixty Million Loan was taken on the head of Greece by the concurring action of the idealistic aspirations of the public and the very materialistic greed of banks that placed the bonds, the fact remains that Greece was not successful in defending itself: It was able to create its own state, but it was so vulnerable from civil war to legitimatize the imposition of the Bavarian dynasty by foreigners, after the assassination of Count Capodistrias by the opposing faction of the Mavromichalis.

In our time, the issue was all domestic policy: The Greek Government, enjoying the complicity of consensus of an overwhelming social majority, has consciously decided to take the risk of a policy of constant deficits, with which to fuel clienteles, consumption, salaries, as well as a not inconsiderable corruption, knowing full well that when international investors would fear the geometric growth of the absolute value of the debt of the country, it would not have been possible to remedy the situation with the instrument of tax revenues, as the country does not have shoulders robust enough from the industrial point of view. And so again, we see Greece looking askance with the rest of the world, and again are heard stereotypes of national character, which if not racist in the biological sense, are racist in a substantive way, because they make up for a lack of understanding of the dynamics of a phenomenon through a surface characterization.

Apparently there is really a conceptual problem: Why do the Greeks reduce themselves to this state of self-exclusion, triggering

---

[211] About, *La Grèce contemporaine*, page 178.

dynamics whose outcome is necessarily self-destructive? The problem is posed by a recent essay by Rodanthi Tzanelli, dedicated to the Anglo-Hellenic controversies in the era of negotiation about the Independence Loans settlement and the ideology of that time:

> ...the reasons of its re-emergence are still obscure. What was the logic of Greek behavior? Why did the Greeks defy the risk of losing their British and other European investors when they needed them? [...] they fell into the trap of cutting-off the lines of communication between themselves and Europe[212].

In this essay is also sketched an unacceptable solution (though really tempered by doubt): Having examined the controversy of the '60 years of nineteenth century, about which Andreadis did not talk in detail, but just hinted, mentioning the offensive couplets of the *Punch*, Tzanelli assumes that there were a fracture of languages and a dynamic of radical misunderstanding between the English ethic of seriousness and the idea of themselves of the Greeks of that time, because the Greeks conceived themselves in terms of opposition between Christianity and the Ottoman Empire, and therefore would consider themselves legitimate creditors on account of their moral suffering under Turkish rule that lasted centuries, and because of the aid they did not receive during that long story:

> This is how the notion of "debt" was appropriated in Greek culture: the British, as Westerners, bore the stigma of the sinner, because their ancestors did not help Constantinople to survive the siege in 1453[213].

Tzanelli quotes as evidence excerpts from the journalistic controversy in the Greek press of the time, where it is true that we can read variations on the theme of the suffering Greek-Christian-Byzantine civilization with diverse rhetorical focus, but we also find denials of the relevance of these topics for the problem of public debt, which was then a pressing issue. But also if this kind of argument was used in nineteenth-century Greece, the point of view of Tzanelli is not sustainable, since in the second half of the century the culture of the Greeks, like that of every other nation of Europe, was no longer the romantic one of their heroic times, recent but inexorably concluded. If anything, it was peppered with memories and romantic stereotypes that were used to put a mask on the prose of the present, and if necessary, also served for the controversy of the moment. Thinking that the Greeks of that time identified themselves

---

[212] *Unpaid Debts and Duties*, pages 27 and 28

[213] *Unpaid Debts and Duties*, page 20

literally with the part of the Christian saviour, or of Christian and Byzantine victims, would be as incongruous as to believe that the Italians and other Europeans of that time identified themselves with the Middle Age characters of the popular literature of that time — maybe the Italians with Marco Visconti and the British with Ivanhoe. The Greeks certainly kept alive a Christian-romantic-styled discourse dating at the time of Philhellenism, and used them in the game played with the British to negotiate better conditions in the adjustment of their position. However, they were not immersed in such a literal pre-modern naivety that their idea of themselves was limited to the image of themselves as oppressed Christians. Tzanelli's essay reflects a common and recurring error in the anthropological perspective: the multiple and contradictory cultural relics that are always present in every place and time are taken in exchange for the authentic cultural institutions, for the representations that a given historical moment actually accepts as categories, because it is not able to achieve any critical abstraction from them.

Actually, the problem of Greece is only that in that country occur phenomena which are associated with their age and with the trends of the entire world, but which receive an interpretation of uncommon personality. We talk about a country that still speaks the language from which derive about fifty thousand words in our vocabulary, and yet is understood by very few; a country that has seen the reappearance of real civil war with many more occurrences than any other European country, last of them the coup d'état of 1967. A country which had a Communist Party stubborn to want the revolution after the war despite the agreements of Yalta, and disobeying the Soviet Union at the cost of its own destruction. Ultimately it is a country that has always disappointed expectations on its economic growth, and yet it is also cut off from land communication with the European continent. So, here the problem seems to be also that of overestimation of its possibilities by all partners.

Given the Greek uniqueness, and when the phenomena of modern Greek history clamour for the world's attention because they become significant for the global equilibrium, as in the case of debt default that is taking place in the spring of this year, the problem is to determine historically with maximum accuracy the internal dynamics of what happens, and not to expect more. The unique personality of the Greek nation makes us fall into the trap of thinking that when a problem is Greek, we should find a special explanatory category of reference; and, since we do not find it, we get into racist-like trivialities, not unlike the *Punch* and the British press in the 60' years of nineteenth century, or the *Bild Zeitung* of these days.

But the Greek debt story, like all phenomena of this world, must be determined historically until the events appear to us motivated, because we recognize the common humanity shared by actors and spectators. The story that we read in this book makes us take a step forward, because it shows how Greece of the Independence War time had become capable of being recognized as a partner on an equal footing by Europe, but then lacked the sufficient experience to administer the credit that it received.

Appendix: Effective Interest on Independence Loans

In the case of the first Independence Loan, the Greeks received a net sum of 348,800 Pounds, and in exchange for this, they had to pay 34 annual instalments of 48,000 Pounds, starting from the third year. At the end the loan it would be repaid, because the contract included an annual fee of 1% amortization. The effective rate, including amortization, is exactly 10.86092509%, applied which for each year and subtracting the instalment in each period, we come to zero in 34 instalments:

Instalment	Capital residue after paying the previous instalment	Years until the payment of next instalment	Debt before the payment of the instalment $C_n=C_0(1+i)^n$ with i = 0.108609509
	348,800.00	3	475,238.89
1	427,238.89	1	473,640.98
2	425,640.98	1	471,869.53
3	423,869.53	1	469,905.68
4	421,905.68	1	467,728.54
5	419,728.54	1	465,314.95
6	417,314.95	1	462,639.21
7	414,639.21	1	459,672.87
8	411,672.87	1	456,384.35
9	408,384.35	1	452,738.67
10	404,738.67	1	448,697.03
11	400,697.03	1	444,216.43
12	396,216.43	1	439,249.20
13	391,249.20	1	433,742.49
14	385,742.49	1	427,637.69
15	379,637.69	1	420,869.85
16	372,869.85	1	413,366.97
17	365,366.97	1	405,049.20
18	357,049.20	1	395,828.05
19	347,828.05	1	385,605.39
20	337,605.39	1	374,272.46
21	326,272.46	1	361,708.67
22	313,708.67	1	347,780.33
23	299,780.33	1	332,339.25
24	284,339.25	1	315,221.12
25	267,221.12	1	296,243.80
26	248,243.80	1	275,205.38
27	227,205.38	1	251,881.98
28	203,881.98	1	226,025.45
29	178,025.45	1	197,360.67
30	149,360.67	1	165,582.61
31	117,582.61	1	130,353.17
32	82,353.17	1	91,297.49
33	43,297.49	1	48,000.00
34	0.00		

Tab. 11

On all loans, to the interest rate of 5% was added another 1% by way of amortization, and so the loan was considered repaid after 36 years. The reasoning was this: The return of 1% of the capital after the first year would make the sum available to be reinvested elsewhere at 5% for 35 years, and applying the compound interest, it would be multiplied by 5.52. The same happens the second year, whose 1% of the capital gives compound interest for 34 years and is multiplied by 5.25 and so on, until the last instalment — fruitless. The sum of the capital shares so returned was considered equal to 100%, but accurate calculation shows it is a little lower, i.e., equal to 95.84:

Multiplication factor	After years	Summation
5.52	35	95.84
5.25	34	90.32
5.00	33	85.07
4.76	32	80.06
4.54	31	75.30
4.32	30	70.76
4.12	29	66.44
3.92	28	62.32
3.73	27	58.40
3.56	26	54.67
3.39	25	51.11
3.23	24	47.73
3.07	23	44.50
2.93	22	41.43
2.79	21	38.51
2.65	20	35.72
2.53	19	33.07
2.41	18	30.54
2.29	17	28.13
2.18	16	25.84
2.08	15	23.66
1.98	14	21.58
1.89	13	19.60
1.80	12	17.71
1.71	11	15.92
1.63	10	14.21
1.55	9	12.58
1.48	8	11.03
1.41	7	9.55
1.34	6	8.14
1.28	5	6.80
1.22	4	5.53
1.16	3	4.31
1.10	2	3.15
1.05	1	2.05
1.00	0	1.00

Tab. 12

The Sixty Million Loan, which was placed at a price of 94% and then reduced by the usual commission, applying the same method appears subject to the effective interest of 5.63%, inclusive of amortization: In fact, to pay back an actual capital of 920,000 Francs (nominal one million), 36 instalments of 60,000 Francs were paid.

Bibliography

Bibliography of the volume of 1904

This is the bibliography of volume of Andreadis. The Greek part has been reproduced without transliteration, as it is clear that those who want to read the quoted works need to be able to read Greek. In the text of 1904 the polyphonic accentuation system is used, but it is replaced here by the simple tonic accent, according to established usage of the last thirty years.

Greek literature

- *Αιών* (Εφημερίς, ο), Φύλλα 1ης και 9ης Αυγούστου 1880.

- Βαλαωρίτης (Ι. Α.), *Ιστορία της Εθνικής Τραπέζης της Ελλάδος*, Αθήναι, 1901.

- Γενναδίου (Ι.), *Έκθεσις 17/29 Δεκεμβρίου 1875.*

- Εισήγησις της επιτροπής της Βουλής περί των νομοσχεδίων των στρατιωτικών και ναυτικών συντάξεων (Νόμοι 2ας και 12ης Φεβρουαρίου 1859), 11 Δεκεμβρίου 1858.

- *Εθνοφύλαξ* (Εφημερίς, ο), Φύλλα 25ης Οκτ. 1863 και 8ης Αυγούστου 1880.

- Έκθεσις της επιτροπής της Γερουσίας (Εισηγητής Χατζίσκος) περί του δανείου των εξήκοντα εκατομμυρίων, 8 Μαρτίου 1860.

- Έκθεσις λογιστική περί του γενικού λογαριασμού των μετατραπέντων δανείων του 1824 και 1825, Αθήναι 1890.

- *Εφημερίς της Κυβερνήσεως* (Συλλογή του φύλλου).

- *Εστία* (Εφημερίς, η), Φύλλον 2ας Απριλίου 1904.

- *Ημέρα* (Εφημερίς, η), Φύλλον 14/26ης Ιουνίου 1872.

- *Ιστορικόν Αρχείον Ρώμα*, μετά προλόγου του εκδίδοντος Δ. Γρ. Καμπούρογλου, Αθήναι 1901.

- Καλλιγάς (Παύλος), *Θάνος Βλέκας*, μυθιστορία (ανεδημοσιεύθη εκ της Πανδώρας του 1855 εν τη Εθνική Βιβλιοθήκη του Γ. Μπαρτ, ά. η.)

- Καλλιγάς (Παύλος), *Λόγος 11ης Δεκεμβρίου 1880 περί Κυρώσεως της συμβάσεως των Βαυαρικών δανείων* (ανεδημοσιεύθη εν *Μελέταις και Λόγοις*, τόμ. β')

- Καμπούρογλου, Δημήτριος Γρ., *Ιστορικόν Αρχείον Διονυσίου Ρώμα*, μετ' εισαγωγής του εκδίδοντος Δ. Γρ. Καμπούρογλου, Athens, 1901 – 1906

- Κανάρης (Κωνσταντίνος), *Έκθεσις εισηγητική της 26ης Απριλίου*

1846 περί του προϋπολογισμού του Υπουργείου των Ναυτικών (εν τω ψηφισθέντι προϋπολογισμώ του 1845).

- Κοντόσταυλος (Α.), *Τα περί των εν Αμερική ναυπηγηθεισών φρεγατών*, Αθήναι, 1855

- Κορεσίου (Ν. Θ.), *Υπόμνημα περί Αγγλοελληνικών δανείων*, Αλεξάνδρεια, 1868.

- Κορφιωτάκη (τότε Υπουργού Οικον.), *Έκθεσις περί του προϋπολογισμού του 1848.*

- Κυριακίδης (Επ.), *Ιστορία του Συγχρόνου Ελληνισμού* (1832, 1892), 2 τόμοι, Αθήναι 1892.

- *Λευκή Βίβλος, Μετατροπή των δανείων του 1824 και 1825*, Αθήναι, 1879.

- Λεβέντης (Α.), *Περί του δημοσίου των Ελλήνων χρέους του 1824 και 1825 και περί νέου δανείου*, Αθήναι, 1865.

- Μάμουκα (Ανδρ. Ζ.), *Τα κατά την Αναγέννησιν της Ελλάδος, ήτοι συλλογή των περί την αναγεννωμένην Ελλάδα πολιτευμάτων, νόμων και άλλων επισήμων πράξεων από του 1821 μέχρι τέλους του 1832*, 11 τόμοι, Αθήναι 1839, 1852.

- Μένδελσων, Βαρθόλδης (Κ), *Ιστορία της Ελλάδος, από της εν έτει 1453 αλώσεως της Κωνσταντινουπόλεως υπό των Τούρκων μέχρι των καθ' ημάς χρόνων*, 2 τόμοι, ελληνική μετάφρασις Αγγέλου Βλάχου, Αθήναι 1873, 1876, which translates: Mendelssohn-Bartholdy, Karl, *Geschichte Griechenlands von der Eroberung Konstantinopels durch die Türken im Jahre 1453 bis auf unsere Tage*, Bd. 1–2, Leipzig, 1870-1874.

- Μεταξά (Α.), *Γενικοί Λογαριασμοί του Κράτους υπό Ιανουαρίου 1833 μέχρι Δεκεμβρίου 1843* (Έκθεσις λογιστική), Αθήναι, 1849.

- Μήλιος (Σπ.), *Αγόρευσις εν τη Γερουσία περί της χρήσεως του δανείου των εξήκοντα εκατομμυρίων* (23 Μαρτίου, 1860).

- Ορλάνδου (Αν.), *Ναυτικά*, 2 τόμοι, Αθήναι 1869.

- Ορλάνδου (Ιω. και Ανδρ. Λουριώτου), *Απολογία εις την κατ' αυτών εκδοθείσαν απόφασιν του Ελεγκτικού Συνεδρίου*, 2 τόμοι, Αθήναι 1839, 1840.

- Παλαμήδης (Ρήγας), *Αγόρευσις προ της Γερουσίας περί της Φάλαγγος και της διαλύσεως αυτής* (8 Οκτωβρίου 1856).

- Παπαρρηγόπουλος (Κ.), *Ιστορία του Ελληνικού έθνους*, 5 τόμοι, γ' έκδοσις, Αθήναι 1896.

- *Πρακτικά της εν Προνοία κατ' επανάληψιν δ' Εθνικής των Ελλήνων Συνελεύσεως*, Ναύπλιον. 1832, Πρακτικά Βουλής,

Πρακτικά Γερουσίας.

- *Πρακτικά Συνεδριάσεως 28ης Οκτωβρίου 1868* (Κύρωσις της μετά των κληρονόμων του Όθωνος συμβάσεως· λόγοι Π. Δηλιγιάννη. Βαλασσοπούλου κτλ.).

- Σπανιολάκης (Γ.), *Παρατηρήσεις επί της Απολογίας Ι. Ορλάνδου και Α. Λουριώτου*, Αθήναι, 1840.

- Τρικούπης (Σπ.), *Ιστορία της Ελληνικής Επαναστάσεως*, 4 τόμοι, α' έκδοσις Λονδίνον, 1853, 1857, γ' έκδοσις Αθήναι, 1888.

- Χρηστίδης, *Αγόρευσις προ της Γερουσίας περί του κανονισμού του δανείου των εξήκοντα εκατομμυρίων* (22 Μαρτίου 1860).

Foreign literature

- About (Edmond), *La Grèce Contemporaine*, 4° ed., Paris, 1860.

- Bayard (William), *An exposition of the conduct of the two houses of G. G. and S. Howland and Le Roy, Bayard and Co, in relation to the two frigates Liberator and Hope*. In answer to a Narrative on that subject by Mr. Alexander Contostavlos, New York, 1826.

- Blaquière (Edward), *The Greek Revolution, its Origin and Progress together with some remarks on the religion, national character etc. in Greece*, London, 1824.

- Blaquière (Edward), *Narrative of a Second Visit to Greece*, including facts connected with the last days of Lord Byron, extracts from correspondence, official documents etc., London, 1825

- Broglie (Duc de), "Discours du 8 Mai sur le projet de loi relatif à l'emprunt grec" (in *Ecrits et discours*, vol. 2).

- Bulwer (H. Lytton), *An Autumn in Greece, comprising sketches of the character, customs and scenery of the Country*. In letters addressed to C. B. Sheridan, London, 1826.

- Circular of the committee of Greek Bondholders, 7 novembre 1862, London.

- Contostavlos (A.), *A narrative of the material facts in relation with the building of the two frigates*, 1° ed. New York. 1826, 2° ed. with a postcriptum by R. Sedgwick, 1826.

- *Correspondence respecting the failure of the Greek Government to provide for the payment of the interest and sinking fund of the Greek Loan*, London, 1846.

- *Daily News*, Issue of 11 October 1878.

- *Discussion à la Chambre des Députés d'Athènes (Une)*, Athens,

1845.

- Drucker (Louis), *An appeal to the Governments and monarchs of Europe.* Quelques documents relatifs aux emprunts helléniques contractés à l' étranger, 1e série, La Haye 1874. — 2e série, Leide 1877.

- Duer (J. e R. Sedgwick), *An examination of the controversies between the Greek Deputies and two mercantile houses of New York*, New York, 1826.

- Economicus, *A letter to The Times on the Greek Debt* (10 November 1875).

- *Economist (the)*, issue of October 1878.

- Fabre (Auguste), *Histoire du Siège de Missolonghi, avec des pièces justificatives*, Paris, 1827.

- *Financier (the)*, Numero del 18 giugno 1877.

- Finlay (G.), *History of the Greek Revolution.* 2 volumes, Oxford 1861 and 1877.

- *General Report of the Commission appointed in Athens to examine into the financial condition of Greece*, London, 1860.

- Gervinus (Georg Gottfried), *Insurrection et Régénération de la Grèce*, French translation Paris 1863. Translates *Aufstand und Wiedergeburt von Griechenland*, 1861-1862.

- Gèorgiades, *La Grèce Economique et Financière en 1893* (Réponse à M. Law), Paris 1893.

- Gladstone (Edward), Declarations at the House of Commons about the Sixty Million Loan, 22 March 1869.

- Gordon, Thomas, *History of the Greek Revolution*, 2° ed., 2 volumes London, 1844.

- Goussios (P.), *Etude sur l'état financier de la Grèce*, accompagnée d'une traduction du rapport de M. Jannopoulos, ministre des finances, à S. M. le roi Georges, Paris 1864.

- *Greek Loans of 1824, 1825 (The)*, How they were handled and what the world thought of, London. 1878. Edited by G. Gennadios.

- Guerin (at the time French ambassador in Greece), *Note sur l'armée grecque* (included in Leconte pp. 155 - 164).

- Haleswood (Edward), *A letter to his Excellency A. Coumoundouros, Minister of finance in Greece*, 27 August 1858.

- Jannopoulos (see Goussios).

- Jourdain, *Mémoires Historiques et Militaires sur les événements de Grèce depuis 1822 jusqu'au combat de Navarin*, 2 volumes, Paris, 1828.

- Law (E. F. G.), *Report on the present economical and financial position in Greece* Annual Series n° 1169, London. 1893.

- Leconte (Casimir), *Étude Économique de la Grèce*, Paris, 1847.

- Leroy, Beaulieu (P.), *Traité de la Science des Finances*, 5° ed., Paris 1899.

- *Livre Jaune* 1866, Paris, 1866.

- *Livre Jaune*, (Arrangement financier avec la Grèce), Paris 1898.

- Monicault (G. de), *Le traité de Paris et ses Suites* (1856, 1871), Paris 1898.

- Odysseus, *Turkey in Europe*, London, 1900.

- Oriental Herald, No 37. (London, January 1826).

- Palma (Alerino), *Greece Vindicated in Two Letters*; to which are added by the same author critical remarks on the works recently published on the same subject by Bulwer, Emerson, Pecchio etc., London 1826.

- Palma (Alerino), "Report on the building of the two frigates" (in *The Times* of 12 September 1826)

- Palmerston (Lord), Speech at the House of Commons, 1 August 1845.

- *Papers relating to the third instalment of the Greek Loan*, 1835, 1836, Presented to the House of Commons by Command of His Majesty, July 1836.

- *Additional papers on the third instalment of the Greek Loan*, 1835, 1836, Presented to both Houses of Parliament, August 1836.

- *Papers relating to the Arrangemement concluded in Athens in June 1860, respecting the Greek Loan*, Presented to the House of Commons in pursuance of their Address dated 29 April 1864.

- Parish (Henry Headley), *The Diplomatic History of the Greek Monarchy from the Year 1830*; showing the transfer to Russia of the mortgage held by British capitalists over its properties and revenues, London 1838.

- Parliamentary Debates 1845 (ed. Hansard), London 1846.

- Peel (Sir Robert), Discorso alla Camera dei Comuni, 1 Agosto 1845.

- Politis (N. E.), *Les emprunts d'états en droit international*, Paris, 1894.

- *Punch (the)*, 3 December 1863.

- *Renseignements sur la Grèce et l'administration du Cte Capodistrias*, par un témoin oculaire des faits qu'il rapporte (Viaros Kapodistrias), Paris, 1832.

- *Report of the evidence and reasons of the award between J. Orlandos and A. Louriottis*, Greek deputies on one part and G. G. and S. Howland on the other part, by the Arbitrators, New York, 1826.

- Sarrut, Report on Balmacéda case, *Journal de droit international privé*, 1891.

- Sedgwick (Henry D.), *A vindication of the conduct and character of Henry D. Sedgwick against certain charges made by the honourable Jonas Pratt*, New York 1826.

- Sedgwick (Henry D.), *Refutation of the reasons assigned by the arbitrators for their award in the case of the two Greek Frigates*, New York, 1826.

- Sicherer (Prof. Hermann von), *Das Bayerisch, Griechische Anlehen aus den Jahren 1835, 1836, 1837* (Ein Rechtsgutachten), Monaco, 1880.

- Stourm (Réné), *Le Budget*, (not identified better, see http://gallica.bnf.fr)

- *Times (the)*, issues of 5, 12, 20, 27 September, 23, 24, 26, 27, 28, 30, 31 October, 1, 3, 4, 9, 13 November 1826, 3 December 1863, 23 March 1869, 10 November 1875.

- Thouvenel (M.), *La Grèce du Roi Othon* (Correspondance de M. T. avec sa famille et ses amis, recueillie et publiée par L. Thouvenel), Paris, 1890.

Bibliography added by the editor

The site http://anemi.lib.uoc.gr, University of Crete, contains numerous books and documents about the Greek Independence in PDF format. Many of the materials quoted by the author can be found there, and from there come the information necessary to integrate certain gaps in the bibliography of the author. Other volumes in PDF format can be found in *Google Books*.

1. Works mentioned by the author, but absent in his bibliography

- Μενδελσώνος Βαρθόλδη, Καρόλου, *Ιστορία της Ελληνικής*

Επαναστάσεως, μετάφρασις Ηλία Ι. Οικονομοπούλου, 1894.

- Μενδελσώνος Βαρθόλδη, Καρόλου, *Οι περί ελευθερίας της Κρήτης αγώνες*, 1891.

- Mendelssohn-Bartholdy, Karl, *Geschichte Griechenlands von der Eroberung Konstantinopels durch die Türken im Jahre 1453 bis auf unsere Tage*, Bd. 1–2, Leipzig, 1870-1874.

- Trost, *Ludwig, König Ludwig I. von Bayern in seinen Briefen an seinen Sohn, den König Othon von Griechenland*, Bamberg, C.C. Buchner, 1891.

2. *Other quoted works*

- Cochrane, George, *Wandering in Greece*, 2 volumes, London, 1837. Memoir book of Cochrane, whose exploits are narrated in chapter A.2.2.2. Ignored by the author.

- Clogg, Richard, *A short History of modern Greece*, 1979, 1986, trad. it. Bompiani, 1996.

- Tzanelli, Rodanthi, *Unpaid Debts and Duties: hegemony, reciprocity and resistance in Greek-European cultural exchange*, http://www.sociology.leeds.ac.uk/assets/files/research/cers/debts -duties-Greek-euro.pdf

Back cover

Back cover

This is a story written in 1904, which tells the vicissitudes of the Greek public debt since its own absolute beginning in 1824. At present this book, more than one hundred years old, is also a modern book, in its own way: We do not know today if the new Greek state failure will be driven civilly by the International Banking System and the European Union, or if it will happen more dramatically, in the form of disordered default. In any case, we can call the story once more "une lamentable histoire," as was qualified by a French businessman, who conducted research about the Greek economy with insight and precision back in 1847.

Our author, Andreadis, intended to tell us the whole story, including the one of the institution of the International Control in 1897, but the first volume translated here was then the only one, and it tells us about two ancient events: the *Independence Loans* that the provisional Greek Government contracted with the private market in London in 1824 and 1825, and the loan of an ill-advised entity that the Government of the new state contracted after 1832, remaining indebted to the Governments of the three Protecting Powers: England, France and Russia. The *lamentable histoire* of this prehistoric part of the story gives us the unique opportunity to understand the structure of a phenomenon of financial catastrophe reduced to its skeleton, almost as if we had been able to make a culture *in vitro* of it.

Andreas Andreadis

Andreas Andreadis (1876 - 1935), a native of Corfu, studied law and economics in Paris and London, then taught economics and public finance at the University of Athens. He was an adviser of Eleftherios Venizelos, but he did not want to have political responsibilities, although on several occasions the ministries of Foreign Affairs and Economy had been offered him. He wrote about economic history: *History of the Bank of England* (1904), *Economic History of Greece from antiquity to modern times* (1918), and was popular for a long time as theatre critic under the pseudonym *Alk*.

www.ingramcontent.com/pod-product-compliance
Lightning Source LLC
LaVergne TN
LVHW091512170726
843492LV00001B/462